EARS ON FIRE

Ears on Fire
Snapshot Essays in a World of Poets

Gary Mex Glazner

LA ALAMEDA PRESS   ALBUQUERQUE

"Mystic Barber of Selçuk," appeared on Salon.com and was selected by NPR's All Things Considered. An early version of "She Holds the River in her Throat," appeared in the anthology *Voices Along the River*, published by The Connecticut Department of Environmental Protection's Kellogg Environmental Center. "Por Que Lorca Ha Muerto," was the runner up in the Concurso de Poesía, La Maison de France, Theme: Federico García Lorca, Granada Spain—celebrating the 100th anniversary of Lorca's birth. "Tea," and "Spooning" appeared on Cleansheets.com and also in *The Underwood Review VOL 3, Number 1*, published by Hanover Press. "Geraldo and the Surfing Buddhas" appeared on Gettingit.com. "Oracle of Delphi," appeared in the anthology *Knowing Stones*, published by John Gordon Burke Publisher, Inc. "Doors," was published by *The Harwood Review*. Many thanks to the publishers and editors.

Some of these poems were performed and shaped at: City Lights Bookstore, San Francisco; The National Poetry Slam; Chicago Theater, Chicago; Poetry Olympics, Rinkabye Cultural Hall, Stockholm; St. Mark's Poetry Project, New York; The Seattle Poetry Festival, Seattle; Shakespeare and Company Bookstore, Paris; Shilendra's garden with the Royal Nepali Poets, Kathmandu; The Texas Book Festival, Austin; The Tucson Poetry Festival, Tucson. The author offers his thanks to the hosts and organizers of those readings.

Special thanks for inspiration to: Sherman Alexie, Pirkko M. Antinoja, Mamdoh Badran, Michael Brown, Leo Butnaru, Andrei Burac, Mats Burman, Miles Davis, Padma Devkota, Paul Devlin, Christine Dimitrova, Shiela Donahue, Sonya Fehér, Don George, Banira Giri, Maria Carmen S. Gonzalez and her mother, Aime Hansen, Mike Henry, Karen Hobson, Bob Holman, Xiong Jinren, Cass King, Xuan Ke, Solja Krapu, Erkki Lappalinen, Eva Leandersson, Roanne Lewis, Eleonora Luthander, Jami Macarty, Don McIver, Anh Ngoc, Wu Rouhai, Marc Smith, Patricia Smith, Eleni Sikelianos, Shilendra K. Singh, Her Royal Highness Princess Maha Chakri Sirindhorn, Thai Ba Tan, The Pink Man, Faith Vicinanza, Ma Quiang, George Whitman, Aaron Yamaguchi, Joanne Young, Leo Zelada, and Ma Zhe.

The first draft of the book was written in Granada, Spain where Maria José Benitez, Daniel Gonzales, Paco Trigo, and Carlos Espejo of the Oxford Bookstore were more than generous in offering the use of their computers and in providing a quiet, warm writing space.

All the photos were taken by Margaret Victor, except the one of her done by the author.

& last—for seeing the book, as it could be, everlasting thanks to J.B. Bryan.

La Alameda Press
9636 Guadalupe Trail NW
Albuquerque, New Mexico 87114

*For companionship, love and muse duties
this book is dedicated to Margaret Victor.*

If we are always arriving and departing,
it is also true that we are eternally anchored.
One's destination is never a place
but rather a new way of looking at things.

Henry Miller
COLOSSUS OF MAROUSSI

Contents

Selected Poets, Books, Festivals and Sites

But we love the Old Travelers.
We love to hear them prate and drivel and lie...
— **Mark Twain**

Travel is the realm of the improbable adventure, the quick fix, the ship passing in the night. It entitles you to meet interesting people, whom you would never meet, even if you laid traps or advertised for them. Not only do you meet them, but also unmeet them, all in the space of, it often seems, a mere compacted evening. As there is so little time, bodies in motion drop their guard and immediately get on with their stories. Then the proverbial ships part, each to its destination, never again to brush each other's wake.
— **Lawrence Millman**

What childishness is it that while there's breath of life
in our bodies, we are determined to rush
to see the sun the other way around?
— **Elizabeth Bishop**

These spiritual windowshoppers,
who idly ask, 'How much is that?' Oh, I'm just looking.
They handle a hundred items and put them down,
shadows with no capital.
What is spent is love and two eyes wet with weeping.
But these walk into a shop,
and their whole lives pass suddenly in that moment,
in that shop.
Where did you go? 'Nowhere.'
What did you have to eat? 'Nothing much.'
Even if you don't know what you want,
buy *something*, to be part of the exchanging flow.
Start a huge, foolish project,
like Noah.
It makes absolutely no difference
what people think of you.
— **Rumi**

If you come to a fork in the road, take it.
— **Yogi Berra**

Foreword

The job I want is poet. On January 2nd 1998 the sale closed, bringing to an end my almost two decades of being a florist. Earlier in my life I had been among other things: boy janitor, chain-wearing disco-pants clothing clerk, green-horn ranch-hand, ink-covered printer, dorm-cafeteria vegetable-chopper, tone-deaf guitar student, hammer-challenged hot-tub builder and unpaid DJ of the "Spank Your Monkey Blues Hour." But most of my life I had spent as flower wrangler. Starting as delivery boy, then clerk, designer, head designer, and manager, finally buying the store on credit and paying it off. All the while writing poems, giving readings and hoping. The sale of the store would allow me to begin to pursue my dream of being a full-time working poet. The idea was to travel around the world of poetry, meet poets, work on translations and write poems

My wife, Margaret, and I traveled approximately 34,229 miles by planes, trains, tuk-tuks, bemos, ferries, broken down Chinese night buses, and rickshaws. We visited Thailand, Nepal, Vietnam, China, England, Holland, Turkey, Greece, Italy, Austria, Hungary, The Czech Republic, Germany, Denmark, Sweden, France, Spain, and Portugal.

The plan had taken root seven years earlier on Gilli Air, a small island off Lombac, below Bali, in Indonesia. We were having dinner with a couple from Switzerland, who were on their own one-year journey around the world. We were amazed they could carry everything for such a long trip in their backpacks. Impressed that they had quit their jobs, left everything. We drank one bottle of banana wine after another, listening to their stories. As the evening went on, it was as if they had brought us with them. After dinner, we walked the few feet to the beach to lie down in the sand. The stars were insatiable, touching everything. It was a seduction, this perfect moment that led to our pact, that someday, we too would close one last door and walk out into the world.

The Real Work of Flowers

The flowers in a casket spray talk. They tell you about the dead.
She was a mother of nine, whose children had stopped speaking to her.
No one knows why she killed herself.
Give her daisies, she loved daisies.
He was a liar, but patriotic, give him red, white and blue carnations.
Who cares? No one will come to the service anyway.

When you're bored you can imagine anything, even taking advice from flowers. When they are blooming they say, "get out while you can." I worked as a florist but I always wanted to be a poet, that is why I trusted the flowers and listened. You can't be a poet everyone says, "there is no money in poetry." Flowers don't know logic. "Sell the store," they say, "travel the world and rewrite Moby Dick only poetry is the whale."

Make an all cash sale and give yourself a grant. Use the time to write poetry. Find out how people make poems, ask them if poetry has a place in their lives. Then the flowers would get gushy and start talking about how beautiful poetry is and how nobody writes good flower poems any more and that maybe if I was successful in becoming a poet I would remember them and write some more of that red, red rose stuff.

Florists get up early to get the smartest flowers. Rushing, to beat the other Black Eyed Susans at the flower market. Listening for the scent of advice. Three times a week I would get out of bed between 3 and 5am, and head down to the San Francisco Flower Market. Turning your sleeping hours into waking hours makes you crazy. Stringing garlands of dreams.

Working the same small retail space for 18 years gives you roots, but not nourishment. The phone rings, the taxes are due, someone thought that ivory was the same as peach. The bride is crying, the deceased hated purple, the delivery person has stolen the gasoline credit card and bought $100 dollars worth of ice cream and is keeping it cool and hidden in the back of the refrigerated truck. Flowers wilt and ruin lives, ruin birthdays, ruin that special moment, there is no forgiveness for wilting.

I put the store up for sale, found a guy who wanted to buy up a string of mom and pop florist shops and pursue the late 90's gold rush; taking them public with an IPO. This guy was all stamen. Pollinating money. No matter that everyone told him, you can't get rich on nosegays. Bouquets are hard work. The people who buy posies are full of emotion, love or death and they take it out on you. Make you feel like you built the dog house and leashed them to its chain. "How big of a bouquet should I buy?" The customers would inquire. Always came the answer, only you can judge her madness. Mr. Green Thumb didn't care. He knew he could grow a fortune. He had the edge, Narcissus had his ear.

Flowers are on the side of poetry and helped close the deal. Outside of the shop, flowers do their real work, silent, pretty, fragrant, covering up the smell of the dead.

> Heads drooping, you bow.
> Black water root.
> Color gone from smell.
> Earth pulling to seed.
> Folded brittle stem,
> crinkled hanging
> collapsing with
> weight of bloom.
> I forgive you,
> for growing old.
> Hang you
> in a dark
> place,
> until
> you are
> perfect.

The Real Work of Flowers

The surprising part of working with flowers was the openness people had with you. As if florist was part therapist. Customers would tell you the most intimate details of their lives and want you to match a color or scent to the revelation. Bouncing between births, deaths, affairs, weddings, and everyday love the florists feels the rhythm of the town. The connection between this rhythm and poetry is most evident when it comes to the signing of the card, often the customer would be a loss for words and plead for you to help, "Come on you know what to say."

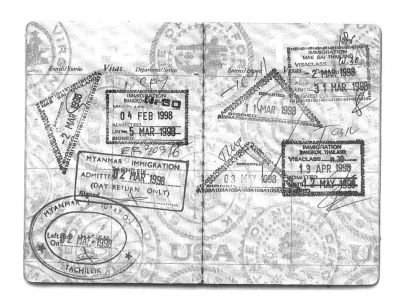

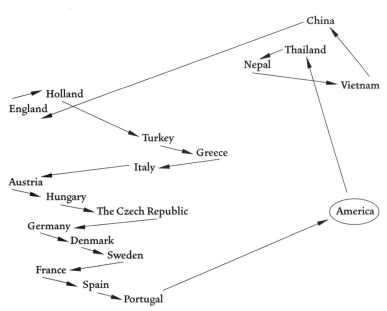

Dear Bangkok,

Are you hot? This is the letter everyone hates to write. I don't love you any more &
never have really. It isn't the traffic or the way you are always late. Forget about the
cabbies driving in circles to jack up the fare. Don't worry about how long it takes
you to come. The air in the mouth of a cave and the mouth of a mall are all the
same. It's not your fired bugs. I just woke up one day, went running through your
streets. Jet lagged dark alleys. Boy/girl grabbing my wrist, pulling me to the
nearest bar. Forget the weird way you kiss. Who taught you to kiss? Some jock
solider, from a war everyone but the winner has forgotten? This is what you call
love—throwing water, getting everything that moves wet. Listen, I don't even
have to explain myself, it's over. Why do you let every German have his way? Why
do you slut your beaches? Who's Leo? Why don't you cover yourself up and get
over it. Oh, stop crying, this is goodbye. I don't want a silk suit. I hate rice. You
can't even feed your fucking elephants. They stand in front of the 7/11 begging for
sugar cane. They beg real good. Up your pointy gold temple. When that monk
slapped me in the head with a bundle of sacred-stupid incense I saw the Buddha
in you. Wave your shiny banners. Sweat into the night. Nothing can cool you off.
You're so hot and busy. I am missing you Bangkok, but not how you want it.
Certainly not the stink of your ping pong balls.

Love,
Noel Coward

Inches from My Face

We would often change our travel plans on a whim. Meeting that couple from Toronto at the beach in Thailand and hearing their love of Nepal, we dropped our plan to go to Malaysia. Booked a flight to Nepal. Kathmandu that's where we're really, really going to. There never was a real plan. We had bought a one-way ticket to Bangkok. Just saying it now gets me all hot. One-way ticket, no return, always into the future.

Being a child of the 1970's I have some pretty weird songs running through my head. On this trip I often sang Stepenwolf's, "Born to Ride," swirling in my brain, "Head out on the highway. Looking for adventure. Whatever comes my way." A sexy walk would trigger this, a floating scent of fried food, a glint of the surface of an umbrella cocktail. Once I sang it to a monkey as he scrambled up a palm tree in search of the missing link.

I am deathly afraid of elephants. I did not discover this until visiting the elephant camp. A woman was petting an elephant, rubbing near his eye, saying how cute he was. The elephant whacked her with his trunk, sent her flying. Everyone was stunned. The mahoot (the elephant keeper), shouted at the elephant, "Bad elephant." People rushed to help the woman up; she was shaken but not hurt. Later after the elephant show, I felt a nudging on my arm. I looked to see who was tapping me. You know how the story ends. Seeing the great gray head inches from my face, I jumped and shouted. Bringing laughter to everyone around, especially Margaret, she watched the beast approach me, without saying a word.

The Case of the Princess Poet

"The Princess allows you to do your work."

This magical decree comes after two months of letters and phone calls. Let me go back to the beginning.

It was our first day of our one-year trip around the world. One year of traveling through Asia and Europe, after 18 years of working as a florist. The first day of being a full-time poet. I can't sleep. It is five am; I go into the bathroom to write so I won't wake up Margaret. I write a poem in the voice of a shoe salesman. I draw a still life of the bathroom. I still can't sleep.

I go down to the street to jog, running through the back alleys of Bangkok. I don't want to get lost so I stay close to the hotel. On one of the streets a group of skinny young men dressed as skinny young women grab me by the wrist and try to pull me into a bar. "Why no want drink? You big handsome guy." Now I am able to run much faster.

Back at the hotel Margaret is reading the paper and she shows me an article about the Princess of Thailand's new book of poetry. One of the goals of this trip is to help find poets for the project, "The World of Poetry" produced by Washington Square Films in New York. I want the Princess for the film but how does one approach a Princess?

The great thing about Princesses is they are mythical beings and although they exist, most of us will experience them only in fantasy. We brought the Princess with us, all through Thailand like an imaginary childhood friend she was there when ever we needed her.

On the beach in Ko Chang, a national park above Cambodia, I would say, "I wonder if the Princess likes fried fish and beer?" She sat down with us at a beach restaurant, just two old wooden tables, three ice chests, a bar-b-que wok, and a kitchen consisting of a few boards and buckets. The fish were fresh, the beer icy and the green papaya salad spicy hot. The Princess loved it. After dinner we ran down to the water, floated on our backs and watched the sun sink into the horizon.

The next day we went back and there was a group of Russians with huge bellies burned red from the sun. We knew the Princess would love the Russians and they being without royalty for so long would delight in her. The Russians sang and performed magic tricks. They insisted we all drink the local hooch, which was a large jar full of wood chips, strips of bark and roots, distilled into clear fiery booze. I took one sip and tried to put my glass down but the Russians insisted I finish it. The Princess had to help me back to our hut.

We were staying in a grass hut for two dollars a day, which leaks when it rains, which it does every night. This is the only time I hear the Princess complain, "Now I know why they call it a palace." But she is tough, rolls over and soon begins to snore.

One day I take the Princess snorkeling on the tiny island of Ko Wai. A few feet from the beach begins the most remarkable coral, it is flowing with the water, flexible, intensely bright, a living painting, a waking dream. The Princess is flabbergasted, "Man, I never knew such a world existed, what a trip." For a Princess she was very down to earth.

The Princess never had stomach problems, even when we brought her to eat at the roadside food stalls. She loved the grilled squid. We never could get her to eat the large toasted bugs though. "Too buggy," she always said.

Back in Bangkok it was New Year's day which is celebrated by pouring water on every thing that moves, with buckets, squirt guns, hoses, anything wet. The Princess was very gentle. She had a small jar of water filled with floating orchids. She smiled as she pulled open my shirt and slowly poured the water down my chest. She started laughing when I jumped feeling the ice cold liquid. This was the only time in Bangkok when I enjoyed the heat of the day.

The Princess fit right into my pocket and protected us from evil silk suit salesmen, helped us give directions to the taxi drivers, and most importantly made the all-night bus drivers slow down. Meanwhile back at the palace . . .

I got the call our last day in Thailand, the hotel desk clerk was nervous, she had forgotten to give us the message the first time the Her Royal Highness' secretary, Aryan called. I don't think the budget Hotel Atlanta gets too many calls from the palace.

I went across the street to the pay phone and got Aryan on the line. We exchanged pleasantries and then she hit me with the news,
"The Princess allows you to do your work."
I was taken aback, what did this mean, did she want to be in the movie? I wasn't used to Princess speak. Growing up in America without a Princess, I wasn't sure what to say, so I repeated the phrase,
 "The Princess allows me to do my work?"
"Yes," again firmly, "The Princess allows you to do your work."

"Tell the Princess, thank you, thank you very much."

It seemed the Palace drawbridge was opened just a crack. I went back and got Margaret. We went to the fancy hotel at the end of the Soi, which had two for one happy hour drinks, and ordered banana daiquiris to celebrate.

As we drank I kept laughing and repeating my mantra:

> The Princess allows you to do your work.
> The Princess allows you to do your work.
> The Princess allows you to do your work.

I knew I wasn't in Kansas anymore, sinking into the fat cushioned couch, listening to the pianist play Bach, sucking on my straw, it felt like home.

The Princess Poet
(PHOTOGRAPH FROM THE COVER OF HER BOOK)

CHANG MEI

Sainam (Stream)

HRH Princess Maha Chakri Sirindhorn

translated by Chindarat Samathmankong and Gary Mex Glazner

S
  t
    r
     e
      a
    m

Winter
within reach
winter wind
  blows strongly
cool chill
  appears everywhere
  the north stream   flow
    flooding the rice fields
      my eyes catch the rim of water
    quick flash of thought
    from the river
    my life ebbing flowing
      passing by   passing by
       a sadness rises
     crowning the current
    this life already past
      never repeating   never stopping
      happiness slipping
   current stronger
     every night   every night
      life lost   we die
     from each other
       gone

A

ABOUT ART RELATED ACTIVITIES -AARA-
THE ART CENTER AT MISIEM YIPINTSOI SCULPTURE GARDEN : OUTREACH PROGRAM

กิจกรรมที่
อะเบาท์สตูดิโอ / อะเบาท์คาเฟ่

พฤษภาคม 2541

A

ABOUT ART RELATED ACTIVITIES -AARA-
THE ART CENTER AT MISIEM YIPINTSOI SCULPTURE GARDEN : OUTREACH PROGRAM

activities at
ABOUT STUDIO / ABOUT CAFE

MAY 1998

t-r-i-p-s

ขับขี่.สุ้มผัส.เขียน.ขับเคลื่อน.เดิน.พูด.มอง.
อ่าน.ดม.ฝัน.สนุกสนาน.ฟัง.คิด.รู้สึก.หายใจ
ออก.บินไป.หอบหายใจ.ติดตาม.รวมหัว.
เชื่อมโยง.ติดไฟ.ฝันกลางวัน.หวัง.กิน.
จัดการ.หมุนโทรศัพท์.ดม.ปลดเปลื้อง.ก้าว
ยาว.หายใจเข้า.ถอนหายใจ.สูด.สำลัก.ฟื้นคืน

t-r-i-p-s

ride.touch.write.drive.walk.talk.
look.read.drink.dream.enjoy.
listen.think.feel.exhale.fly.gasp
.follow.conspire.connect.plug-in
.daydream.hope.eat.deal with.
dial.sniff.strip.stride.inhale.
sigh.snort.suffocate.come-round

อะเบาท์สตูดิโอ / อะเบาท์คาเฟ่
402-408 ถนนไมตรีจิตต์ ป้อมปราบ กรุงเทพฯ 10100
โทรศัพท์ 623 1742-3 โทรสาร 623 1743

เวลาเปิด สตูดิโอ :
จันทร์-เสาร์, 10.00 น. - เที่ยงคืน
เวลาเปิด คาเฟ่ :
จันทร์-พฤหัส, 19.00 น. - เที่ยงคืน
ศุกร์ และเสาร์, 19.00 น. - 02.00 น.
ปิดวันอาทิตย์

ABOUT STUDIO / ABOUT CAFE:
402-408 MAITRI CHIT RD., POMPRAP,
BANGKOK 10100
PHONE 623 1742-3, FAX 623 1743
STUDIO HOURS:
MONDAYS-SATURDAYS, 10 AM-MIDNIGHT
CAFE HOURS:
MONDAYS-THURSDAYS, 7 PM-MIDNIGHT
FRIDAYS & SATURDAYS, 7 PM-2AM
SUNDAYS CLOSED

Walking around Bangkok we stumbled into the About Studio/ About Café. They had just had a performance by Ukabat, the performance art group that the Pink Man belongs to. The owner told us about the happening, a combination of poetry and art that involved toothpaste. The café is set up like a living room with funky couches and coffee tables. To complete the Greenwich Village feel they brought us bowls of hot salted soy beans. They gave us directions to the Weekend Market and how to find The Pink Man.

The Pink Man poem excerpt:

The Plastic Flower
Walk, walk, walk, walk, walk, where we walk?
Walking to the modern world destruction.
Walk, walk, walk, walk, walk, where we walk?
Who knows the meaning of life?
I don't know.
I bring flowers to the ladies of the world.
Unfortunate-plastic flowers.
I bring flowers to the gentlemen of the world.
Unfortunate-plastic flowers, I don't want.

Sompong Thawee (1950-)
Sompong Thawee known as "The Pink Man," is a performance poet who dresses in a bright pink silk suit. On the day of Thailand's economic crash in 1997, he handed out pink balloons emblazoned with the name of western corporations and fashion designers. Along with the Brothers Paisarn and Mongkol Plienbangchang, Thawee's ensemble Ukabat are famous for their parody of the Thai tourist campaign, "Amazing Thailand," where he posed in his pink suit in front of cultural icons, rice fields, temples, rural villages, etc.

City of Windows

Kathmandu city of windows.
One eye looking in, one eye looking out.
One eye forgotten, blinded by colors,
rising from Holi streets.

Our first day in Kathmandu was the day of the "Holi Festival." As we walked a narrow street, we heard laughter, then from above a bucket of water poured down. We were drenched. A group of young boys ran up. They were smeared with red from head to toe. In their hands, they held a fist of red powder, which soon found its way to our faces and hair.

One eye looking in, one eye looking out.
Red, blue, silver, gold,
rising from Holi streets.
Raining from children's hands.

Initiated we were part of the party and for an afternoon, we wandered the street providing wonderful targets for the children's water balloons or as they called them, "Lolas." They seemed to find special delight in targeting my wife's bum, saving their best shots for her. An account of the origins of the festival from *The Kathmandu Post:*

> The festival of Fagu or Holi has the myth the Demon King Hiranya Kashyapu ordered his sister Halika to enter a fire with Prahlad, the demon's son a follower of Lord Bishnu, in her lap so that Prahlad could not have chanted prayers in the name of Lord Bishnu with the belief that his sister won't burn herself because she had received a boon that she wouldn't burn in fire. But it so happened that Halika was burned in the fire whereas Prahlad remained safe and alive and came out of the fire chanting prayers in the name of god. From then, onwards the festival is celebrated by smearing colours in enjoyment.

Red, blue, silver, gold.
Rooftops, mountains of laughter
Raining from children's hands.
Lolas bursting with joy.

The next morning we read that a young man had been stabbed when he smeared someone with powder
who had told him to stop.

Rooftops, mountains of laughter.
Dancing life of dust.
Lolas bursting with joy.
Wearing a crown of water.

Dancing dust of life.
One eye forgotten, blinded by color.
Wearing a crown of water.
Kathmandu city of windows.

City of Windows
The Holi Festival was a great introduction to Kathmandu. It was thrilling to be a part of the action instead of watching as a tourist. Still, it had a dark undercurrent and most people stayed inside.

World of Poetry

This report contains some thoughts on working with poetry in different languages, and overviews of the poetry scenes in Nepal and Thailand.

Poetry in Translation:

With modern technology we have a unique opportunity to set new standards for what is thought possible for the translation of poetry. There is a grave potential for poetry to lose strength when translated from its original language. Much of the poetry in Nepal and Thailand I have encountered could benefit from stronger translations or from new methods of presenting translations.

Here are a few ideas for translations, followed by two examples of translation problem areas—

1.   By using HTML for presentation on web sights and CD ROMs it will be possible to hear the poem in the original language while viewing translations in a variety of languages. In addition, showing a literal word for word translation would be helpful in getting at the essence of the poem. It is during the stage of translating grammar from one language to another that the poems often breakdown.

2.   Have poets familiar with the original language and the language the poem is being translated into work with language experts during the translation process. Often the language experts are not familiar with poetry skills such as line breaks and free verse rhythms. If possible work with the poet who composed the work.

3.   Recite poetry to taxi drivers and maids.

4.   Matching poets of different countries to do the performance/reading of the translated work, for example Anne Waldman would be a strong choice to recite Banira Giri's poem, "Kathmandu."

One example of a problem in translation is Sujit Wong Theet's poem, "Love Song to the Prime Minister." "Love Song" is written in an old folk rhythm called *saepa*, which when recited is almost sung with a tone alternating between deep guttural and nasal, with a strong rhythm (imagine an elephant singing through the mouth of a monkey, while dancing on her front legs). Translated into free verse, the poem lacks the qualities of the Thai original.

Another example is the Nepali poem "Blow at Dawn" by Bhupi Sercan. You can see in line 4 {poem on pages 32 & 33} that the Nepali word for "regularly" is "Niamitroompma," although "regularly" certainly works, it has little of the fascinating sound of the Nepali word. During a performance of this poem, I found it possible to draw out some of the language by using a technique I'll call "exploding the poem" or the "Big Bang Po." The process works as such: Read the poem first in Nepali (in performance for a Nepali audience) straight through with emphasis on the clarity of the tones of the words. Then read in English with key phrases and words repeated in English and Nepali. For instance, the line 'Seta seta ujjwal dant," followed by "bright bright white teeth" worked well as a chorus. With the word "Niyamitroopma" I alternated with its English counterpart, working the syllables of "reg-u-lar-ly" to give some of the flavor and rhythm of Nepali. This technique can also be used with two or more voices.

Overview of poetry in Nepal:

Nepal has a strong active poetry community eager to make contact with poets of other countries. Nepal's most famous poet Laksm Prasada Devkota (1909-1959) composed his classic poem, "Muna-Maden" in 1936. A simple love story "Muna-Maden" was written to be recited or sung to an easy (*jhyaure*) folk melody. From the youngest student to the oldest village farmer, an instant kinship would develop by singing a line from this poem. Devkota is greatly loved in Nepal. Imagine a poem that an Oklahoma cotton farmer, a beer drinking Budweiser factory worker, or a Wall-Street-Money-Guy all laugh at and recite along with you, then you have an idea of the response Devkota elicits in Nepal! He sets the mark for all poets.

Last year Nepal held a contest similar to the Poetry Slam. Approx. 1000 Poems where sent in from around the country. Judges selected 100 poems which where then performed by the poets scored on performance and content. The winner was 20 year old Bhupin Vyakul with his poem "Rivers are not Men."

In the eastern part of Nepal (nearest India), the Mushai'ra takes place. It is a modern version of the Agon in which poets compete in recitation; these events are well attended and in the past drew crowds of up to 50,000.

Overview of Poetry in Thailand:

At this time it is difficult to find translations of Thai poetry. The Silapakorn University project is working on 50 English, French, and German translations of modern poems. They are in the last six months of a three-year project. Publications of the poems will be issued over the next few years.

Bangkok has everything from a Princess Poet to a thriving performance/poetry scene with a similar energy to New York. The strongest work is that of the "The Pink Man," the creation of poet Sompong Thawee and director/artist Manit Sriwanichpoom. They have made a video satire of the Thailand Tourist Bureau's "Amazing Thailand" campaign. It includes footage of The Pink Man performing in the streets of Bangkok. Another of their projects is "This Bloodless War," the recreation of famous photos from the Vietnam/American war, as a modern assault of consumer/ capitalism. They display the artwork of framed photographs by having a group of people hold up the art standing in rows parading as art gallery walls. They stand in front of government buildings, outside of shopping malls, or anywhere they can draw a crowd.

World of Poetry

The World of Poetry Reports were sent to Washington Square Films, to help find local poets for their "World of Poetry," project, a continuation of the PBS series, *The United States of Poetry*. Check out www.worldofpoetry.com

The World's Fastest Performance Poet

The girl is singing, teasing the crew. They respond with laughter, we hang in the air. In a slate teahouse, I move away from the circle, the beat of the orange glow, the rhythm of eyes. I have no idea what anyone is saying. The girl is fast, blocking the men. She chants. She curses. They are no match for her, mumbling. Outside the snow, blooming, filling the air. White against the pink fragrance of the rhododendron blossoms.

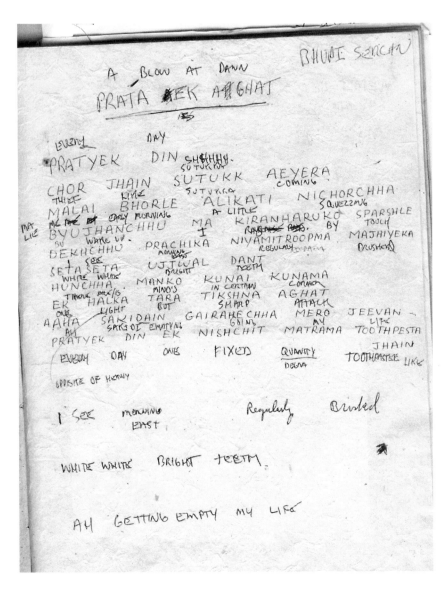

This is a notebook page showing the translation process. Shilendra K. Singh and I would meet at my hotel in the Tamal section of Kathmandu, have soda water and peanuts and work for hours on translations. Shilendra also taught me to recite the poem in Nepali. Whenever I saw one of the maids I would practice the white, white, bright teeth line. What to make of one of the guests constantly complementing your shining smile?

Prata Ek Aghat (A Blow At Dawn)

Bhupi Sercan

translated by Shilendra K. Singh and Gary Mex Glazner

Everyday. Thief like shhhhh coming
me, early morning a little squeezing.
I wake by sunray's touch.
I see the east morning regularly brushed.
White, white bright-teeth.
In a corner of my mind.
One light but sharp attack. Ah emptying, going my life.
Every day fixed quantity toothpaste like.

Bhupi Sercan (1936-1989)
The most influential Nepali poet since Devkota and a communist who wrote under the pseudonym Savahara, (proletariat). A funny and satirical poet who combined classic Nepali with English loan words to great effect.

Shilendra K. Singh

The rickshaw driver is small; his feet barely reach the pedals. Still, we are moving fast through the Kathmandu alleys. The stalls along side the road are full of hanging carcasses, a goat, a cow, chickens, blood dripping, heads chopped off and smiling beside the bodies. The smell of incense and urine fills the air. Someone hacks and spits, then another, and another, as if the sound of spitting reminded everyone that they also needed to spit, loud, rattling, full-bodied spit. Touts creep from the crowds pleading,

> "Hash?"
> "Tiger Balm?"
> "Swiss Army Knife?"

We weave through them. Driver pumping, looking back at me as if I might jump out, ringing his bell, tilting around a car, shouting for the crowd to move. We wheel past cloth embossed with gold and silver, carts of vegetables, bowls of green, blue, orange, and red colored powders, God statues adorned with flowers and smeared with the rainbow of powders. The rickshaw swirls them all, the sounds, the colors, the smells, we are moving through a painting, through a dream, a hallucination, he is taking me to meet a poet, to meet Shilendra K. Singh.

He drops me on Freak Street. I rush up the small dark staircase and show Singh his book *Poems by Nepali Women*, he smiled but said nothing. We removed our shoes and sat down on mats. Another man came into the room. He handed me his card which identified him as, Shilendra L. Singh, writer and editor. One letter off, L. Singh, K. Singh, what does it matter? We laugh and sip hot tea.

Shilendra K. Singh
Imagine someone from another country showing up at your doorstep, barging into your home, only to find out he is looking for someone entirely different. In Nepal, Singh is as common a name as Smith.

Gurka God Dice

Budhe Pun

Three young girls peak out from under their shawls. Behind the girls lies the Delegari mountain range, filling the sky with white. We ask for Mr. Budhe Pun. The girl's mother yells in Nepali, "He's in his cowshed."

We are in the village of Nangi, in the Annapurna region of the Himalayas. The village is in a valley ringed by 15,000 foot plus mountains. This morning, the sky is cloudless with a sting of cold to the air.

The night before I had read a book of folk tales produced by the village school and one of the teachers has agreed to introduce me to Pun, a storyteller and ex-Gurkha solider who served in the British army for 30 years. The Gurkas are legendary fearless fighters, with incredible strength gained as children playing up and down mountain trails.

On the way down to the cowshed, the teacher tells me the school has a web sight with all the folk tales. We have walked for three days, six to eight hours a day, gained thousands of feet in elevation and now I learn I could have stayed home and read the stories on my computer!

We walk down a cobble path to a small stone house with a black slate roof. The teacher calls out. No answer. He goes around back and returns saying, "Pun is milking his cow and will be right out." A few minutes later a short, slight man, not the warrior I had imagined, rounds the corner. We shake hands and I ask if he has time to tell us a story. He laughs and rubs his head. He has been drinking "Roxie," the local rice brew and doubts if he can remember any. Then a boy brings out a straw mat, and we all sit down. Within minutes, he is telling a tale. Surrounded by chickens and cows, sitting on the ground outside the simple house it feels as if we have slipped back hundreds of years. The story goes like this:

"Many, many years ago there was a poor boy without parents. He lived in an old straw hut. He was very hungry but could not get any food. One day the boy went to the cliff and hanging down on the side of the cliff among some rocks was a plant that the boy could eat. He climbed down the cliff and began to eat. When he was finished eating, he realized the trail was too steep to go back up and too steep to go down.

He didn't know what to do, and then he found a cave in which he could take shelter. He went into the cave and began to weep. He knew he would die. How could he get out? He cried even louder. As luck would have it, God was passing the cave and heard the boy crying. God asked why the boy was so full of tears and sorrow.

The boy said, "I came here to eat the plant but now I cannot get down or up and I have no parents. Surely I will die here." So God took pity on the boy and helped him down. Then God said, "Would you like to play a game of dice? You can have three rolls and whatever number comes up, you will be granted that amount of things you have wished for."

The boy rolled a seven and he imagined a palace. Suddenly a great palace appeared with seven floors. He rolled again and the dice came up three. He had imagined riches and there were three piles of gold, silver and jewels. His third roll he wished for love, and six beautiful women appeared. He was as rich and happy as any king.

In the village where the boy lived there was rich man who had heard of the boy's new wealth. The rich man went to visit the boy. He asked him how he became so wealthy. He told the man of how he went to the cliff to find food, how God had helped him and of the rolling of the dice. The man wanted to play the dice game. God came down and gave the man the dice. The man went home to his wife and told her about the game and asked her what he should wish for. His wife didn't believe the man, so she cursed at him and turned away in anger. The rich man was so mad he threw the dice down cursing back at his wife. He became his curse turning into a giant penis, covered with hundreds of smaller penises.

(Pun stops speaking. The four men and women and five children who have gathered, roll with laughter. This is not a story told in mixed company. Embarrassed he begins the tale again).

The rich man throws the dice and wishes all the penises away. But he forgets about one thing and when he turns back into a man, his own penis is gone. Now he has only one roll left, and he wishes his penis back."

The moral of the story; *Beware Gods bearing dice.*

Gurka God Dice
This story took place on a twelve day trek on the Annapurna Trail. We had an entourage of porters led by our guide Mansingh. While talking about our families we told Mansingh the concept of "time-out" in disciplining children. I believe I may be the first person put in "time-out" in the Himalayas.
STORY TRANSLATED BY MANSINGH GURUNG & GARY MEX GLAZNER

Magar

Gathering baskets
of flat gray slate,
to repair
their stone roof home.

Women unearthing
laughter. Singing
the valley
full.

Each mute step

up the trail

wakes a new way

to listen.

Magar
This scene took place on the first day of the trek. Hours later we were in a village drinking Roxie, a strong mullet based liquor. I had a hangover that lasted for days.

Silence of Poetry

"Poetry is a discourse in words of the poet with wordlessness" translates, Padma Devkota. This idea that poetry comes from a play between what can be spoken and what can never be brought into language, comes from Madhav Ghimire. We are at a poetry reading being held in Shilendra K. Singh's garden in Kathmandu, Nepal. Ghimire once served as the Royal Nepali Poet. Padma Devkota is the son of Nepal's favorite son of poetry, Laksmiprasad Devkota. This gathering includes Nepal's best known poets (also present are Toya Gurung, Bhuvan Dhungang, Banira Giri and Tek Karki). The garden is in a shady courtyard off a busy dusty street.

Giri reads her poem "Kathmandu":

> Kathmandu has become a blazing heater
> Of hundreds of thousands of volts;
> Like Sita on the pyre of fire,
> The capital's orphan girls
> Are sitting upon it, ready
> To brand their golden bodies;
> They are trapped by the noose of its love.

Giri lays her words on the canvas of silence that represents the life of women in Nepal. She speaks for them, giving public voice to their sentiments. She portrays the city as a car, the car as symbol of men.

> And is Kathmandu not really a Toyota Corolla
> With white plates
> That gulps down litre upon litre of pertrol but is never satisfied?
> And is this not Nanica's liquor store
> Where crowds of Gunjamans and Ram Bahadurs
> Hold their heads high every day
> And beat their wives when they go home?
> The deep marks of a Toyota's tyres on the street,
> Green bruises from blows struck by Gunjamans and Ram Bahadurs
> All over the women's bodies:
> The daily accomplishments, perhaps, of Kathmandu.

This is a bold jump for a Nepali woman to resist the abuse of violence that is ingrained in her culture. Bold for any woman. Giri continues to explore the balance between the spoken and unspoken.

> Kathmandu is the thing
> My dear son mutters in his dreams;
> Half I understand, half I do not,
> But still I want to hear every moment;
> Surrounded and swamped in past attractions and repulsions,
> I discover
> Many curse me,
> Few like me,
> It seems—
> Though I am living in Kathmandu
> Has Kathmandu somehow not come to live in me?

Switching between, the image of car wheels grinding into the backs of women, to the soft dream image all women will understand; a son talking in his sleep. The mother watching over him, watching over her city, trying to understand, coming to see how much her city makes up her being. She ends with the Napali people and Kathmandu.

> The people of Kathmandu
> Are always singing the vine,
> Always walking the same alleyways,
> Always keeping the same feastdays,
> Always filling the same fairs,
> Always observing the same festivals,
> They are Kakakul birds, chanting
> Kathmandu, Kathmandu,
> Kathmandu, Kathmandu.

Kathmandu catching in her throat as if she were a bird unaware of any meaning of her words but the sound.

Knowing only the basic survival words in Nepali, I hear these poems as pure sound, separated from the intellectual source of their inspiration. It is delightful and disconcerting at the same time. I want to know what they are saying, still it is pleasurable to listen to their voices as one listens to music. Karki's poem, "Dogs Speak English" gives me hope.

Shilendra reads from his poem about discovering what it means to be a Nepali, how he never really felt this until he was standing in line during a trade blockade from India. He catches this in the ending of his poem:

> On a biting hot day of June.
> The sharp smell of the sweat
> of those standing
> so disciplined in their tattered rags.
> When I think of all the speeches
> I gave about Nepalese Nationalism,
> I am ashamed.

Nepal's most famous poet is Laksmiprasad Devkota. His presence is felt through his son? Anytime, anywhere in Nepal that I recited a line from Devkota's classic "Muna Maden" it would bring a smile, a laugh, in an instant we were comrades.

I knew Devkota, they knew me, and we shared this poet. In a taxi in Kathmandu, I sang a line from the poem. The driver laughed and sang with me. Trekking in the Himalayas I shouted to a farmer plowing his field, he smiled and waved, "Devkota!" "Muna Maden" describes the fate of two lovers; Maden like many Nepali men is forced to leave home to find work. Maden travels to Tibet. He experiences many adventures along the way. When Maden finally returns home he finds that Muna has died of a broken heart. One part of the poem that everyone I spoke with mentions is the section were he falls ill on the trail, is abandoned by his companions and is saved by a lower class farmer.

> He who helps his fellow man will surely go to heaven,
> A son of a Chetri, I touch your feet, but I do not touch with distaste,
> A man is a man from the size of his heart, not from his caste[2] .

For a society governed by the caste system, where marriages are arranged according to caste, where a person's choice of occupation is determined at birth, this is a powerful scene showing that artificial distinctions can be overthrown by individual actions.

POETRY READING IN KATHMANDU (*from top left clockwise*): *Margaret Victor, Gary Mex Glazner, Bhuvan Dhungang, Madhau Ghimire, Tek Karki, Tonya Gurung (reading), Padma Devkota.*

PHOTOGRAPH BY SHILENDRA K. SINGH

"Muna Maden" is effective in a country were the literacy rate is low. Devkota based the poem on a Newari ballad and used a form of folk song to compose the poem making it accessible and easy to memorize.

His poem "Mad," starts with:

> I see sounds,
> hear sights,
> and taste smells,
> I touch things thinner than air,
> those things
> whose existence the world denies[3] .

The play between the spoken and the unspoken, between conscious and unconscious, the realm were poetry comes alive. The reading ended with Padma reciting his poem "War and Love":

> Wars scratch with hurricane fingers
> the beauty of the world

Scars the face of history.
Strife and struggles rumble at random.
Power calls from heights that render men means,
beguile them,
turns soldiers into sacrificial lambs.
I seek the safety of my room to pray for everlasting peace,
I seek the safety of my room to pray for everlasting peace,
knowing prayers are of no use.
I refuse to be butchered like a Christ.
For I need to create my own selfish world of love.
Few are sheltered.
Few are saved.
Many emulate the rich confines
that observe and define
the trespassers of my world.
So I seek the safety of my room
to pray for everlasting peace.

[1] "Kathmandu," by Banira Giri. Translated by Michael J. Hutt, *Modern Literary Nepali, An Introductory Reader* (Delhi, Oxford University Press 1997)

[2] "Muna Maden" by Laksmiprasad Devkota. ibid.

[3] "Mad" by Laksmiprasad Devkota. ibid

Laxmi Prasad Devkota *(1909-1966)*
Best known for his poem, "Muna Madan," published in 1935. I asked everyone I met in Nepal about this poem; everyone knew at least a few lines from it. "Muna Madan," is similar to the Vietnamese poem "Tale of Kieu," in this respect. It is heartening to find poetry so well respected and at the center of their cultures.

Banira Giri *(1946-)*
She lives in Kathmandu and teaches Napali at Padma Kanya Campus, Tribhuvan University.

Only Life is Left

Tonight listening to the train grind its way to Hanoi, I remember the village of Hoi An's fishmongers' buzzing voices. Rising and falling along the river as they have for centuries. See her oldest home with the carved wooden scrolls holding Chinese poems. The characters formed of birds, as if the words were flying, their motion held in stillness. The rail cars clacking wheels echoing the funeral procession seen from our hotel balcony. The casket carried on a gaudy gold bus, ornate and festive. At each house they stopped and took off the casket to say goodbye, a last quick visit. A group of mourners walking behind the bus followed by a brass band playing a tireless dissonant dirge. A natural contrast to the wedding at the hotel the day before. Bride in a gown of virgin satin, groom in white tails with a red bow tie. The dress swept down the staircase in the bright camera lights. The flower girls giggling, dreaming of their happy day. A tall thin man from the wedding party turned and our eyes stopped. He seemed to know my face, silent he held my gaze, as if we were exchanging vows.

Enter the Temple of Literature

At lunch Thai Ba Tan tells me, "The poets you shook hands with this morning are hands that have killed Americans. No one else will tell you, we hate you Americans. Our children lived in holes in the ground to escape the bombing. On the surface everyone will be polite, we need your tourist dollars, but inside we can not forget what was done to us."

A few days later he surprises me by inviting us for dinner. An Noc and his daughter are also invited. She translates for her father as he sings a folk lullaby he sung to her when she was a baby.

An Noc and daughter with the author

The Temple of Literature or Van Mieu
Located in Hanoi. Established circa, 1070 A.D. Here are a few lines from the poem, "Improvisation on a Summer Day," by Nguyen Trai (1380 to 1442) who served as a Royal Examiner at Van Mieu: "After so many years of war, only life remains. Half a bed, a breath of clean air, the resting still is good. When may I go build again my home in the shade of apricot trees?"

Improvisation on a Summer Day

after Nguyen Trai

Lying in bed
with the window open
I hear the explosion
of applause.
Hanoi has scored
a goal against Brazil.
All over the city
radios are tuned to
the match, the stadium
a bowl of joy.
Now is the moment,
in apricot shade
to build again
a home.

World of Poetry

This report contains a brief discussion of poetry forms, some comments of the current state of poetry here and poetry highlights.

Enter the Temple of Literature:

The poetry of Vietnam stretches back to pre-recorded history. The oral tradition of blind men singing poems at ferry crossings and markets is still alive. I heard one such poet at a morning market in Hoi Ann. There was a project to record these folk poets of the early 70's by John Balaban.

One of the most well known and loved Vietnamese poets is Nuygen Du, who wrote the "Tale of Kieu." Kieu is a love story based on a Chinese folk tale. There is a similar feeling here that the Nepalese have to Devkota's Muna-Maden. With everyone from street sellers to academics aware of the poem.

The poetry of Vietnam takes 4 main forms: Luc Bat, That Ngon Bat Cu, That Ngon Tu Tuy Et and Tho Moi Luc Bat originated from lullabies and is still sung to the children. It consists of alternating lines of 6 and 8 words or syllables. Rhyming the end word of line 1 with the 6th word of the following 8 word line poems can be of any length, used mostly by uneducated people, farmers ect. Luc Bat is an old form and not many poets use it any more.

That Ngon Bat Cu translates as a poem with 8 lines, 7 words per lines and That Ngon Tu Tuy Et is a poem with 4 lines, 7 words per line. The rhyme pattern is based on falling and rising tones of the end words. These two forms come from the Chinese and were seen as elitist, used by the scholars during the Vietnamses under Chinese rule during the Tang dynasty. Tho Moi is new poetry or free verse. As in the West, most poetry written today is free verse.

Met with Pham Tien Duat, Director of the Vietnam Writer's Association, translator Thai Ba Tan, children's poet Pham Ho, and editor, poet, producer Anh Ngoc early one morning at the association headquarters. Many toasts to poetry with strong rice- based, bourbon-like drink. Blasted by 9am. The poetry scene at this time in Vietnam is incredibly strong. So much so that Tien expressed concern that the art of poetry may be lost. He feels that it is too accessible and easy to be published. Most newspapers print poems on a regular basis. Tien feels that people do not take the time to study and improve their craft. He gave as an example the poetry club in his village, which he belongs to. Tien says that although a tremendous amount of poetry is being composed, that as of now, Vietnam has not produced a major poet of world status. An interesting perspective, with parallels similar to criticisms of the poetry written by Slam Poets.

Poetry highlights:

1. The first broadcast of the Poetry Fan Club on VTV was May 1st, 1998, with the second broadcast set for June 1st. The show includes poetry competition with judges. Anh Ngoc is one of the producers.

2. Anh Ngoc edits a literary magazine for the military, "Vanghê quândôi." It is the oldest magazine in Vietnam.

3. There are 600 members in the Association of Writers.

4. Translations of Shakespeare's Sonnets into Vietnamese by Thai Ba Tan.

Tale of Kieu by Nguyen Du (1765 to 1820), translated by Sanh Thong Huynh, (Yale Univ Press; 1987). This epic poem dates from the seventeenth century and is a cornerstone of Vietnamese literature. Written in popular verse form. The easy rhyming style helps the poem to be memorized even by illiterate people.

Jackfruit

Ho Xuân Huong

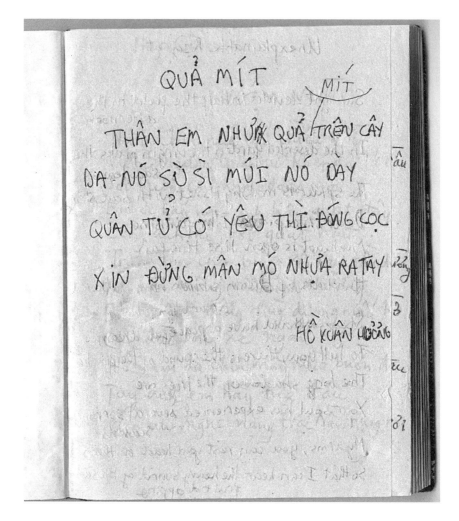

Jack Fruit

Ho Xuan Hong is the new Rumi, equally mystic and funny. She lived in Vietnam from about 1780 to 1825. She was a concubine. Or she didn't exist at all and was the pen name for an embarrassed mandarin. I honed this translation slowly, looking up each work in my Vietnamese-English dictionary and checking the work with the poetry loving desk clerk of our hotel.

Jackfruit

Ho Xuân Huong

translated by Gary Mex Glazner

> My body is sweet as Jackfruit.
> Its bark is rugged, its pulp thick.
> Plant your sword captain, if you like.
> Touch it. Your hands turn wet.

She Holds the River in Her Throat

The cormorant cannot sing.
She holds the river in her throat.
Her neck knotted with noose.
Trident of beak and claws.

She holds the river in her throat.
Who will not swim into her mouth?
Trident of beak and claws.
Is it true she loves the hunt?

Who will not swim into her mouth?
Passion catching the feather of words.
Is it true she shares her empty belly?
Where is my watery book of tide?

Passion calling the feather of words.
Silent in the torchlight.
Where is my sweet fish scent?
Impossible mountains hungry gray wishes.

Silent in the torchlight.
Her neck knotted with noose.
Gone gray with mist.
The cormorant cannot sing.

Fried Grasshopper

Grasshopper shadow
    flying into my belly
        sun wings flutter

Fried Grasshopper
A huge bowl of wiggling green grasshoppers fried to a delicate crisp. French Fries with wings.
Once the Chinese diners found out our desire to join in eating bugs, the beer flowed and flash
bulbs sparked.

Card Playing Monks

The Monks circumnavigate the temple in deep burgundy robes and tasseled banana like hats, chanting in a rolling valley of green grassland and yellow mustard. The rooftops of the temple are covered with gold, or something shining like gold. The village homes made of brown adobe. Visiting Tibetans wear coats with sleeves that hang down dragging in the dirt streets, long knives stuck in their belts. When the Monks need to pee they squat, robes draping and let go. Never talk to a squatting Monk. Welcome to the Wild-Wild East! Xiahe, in the remote hills of northwestern China has the highest concentration of Tibetan monks outside Tibet and houses the Labrang Monastery, the world's largest school of the Yellow Hat Sect of Tibetan Buddhism.

Tourist activities include:
1. Be eaten by wild dogs. Packs of wild dogs roam the hills outside of town. Tourists going for walks in the idyllic, impressionistic landscape would be attacked and torn to pieces by the wild dogs. It was said that the dogs could smell the difference between locals and visitors.
2. Buying long metal dog repellent rods. Which everyone accept the rod salesman said would hardly help you fight off a hungry pack of canines.
3. Eating noodles.
4. Buying cotton candy from the foot pumped cotton candy street machine.
5. Playing cards with gambling Monks.

Enter the land of cheating, screaming Monks. Each day there is a special school session that centers on a group of Monks screaming at a junior Monk. A kind of Monk boot camp exercise. The great thing about screaming is that no translation is needed to see who wins. Shocking as it is to hear the shaved head, religious devotees using full-steam yodeling as a teaching technique, to be hoodwinked in a card game by them reversed all my opinions on the spirit of saintliness. The grinning Monks approached, spread out their cards, dealt me in. It was a flurry. Each time I reached for a card, tried to make a move, to put a Jack with a Queen, or a Spade with a Spade, the game would shift. Suddenly only fives and tens could go together, or Hearts with Clubs. Each

Next stop on the Middle Way—New York City and Three Card Monty

round I lost would send the Monks into deep hearty laughter, the laughter of someone who understands the fickle universe, the laughter of someone with no worldly possessions to gamble away. Those Monks where divining the rules and that made them giggle. Dishonest Monks unable to control their impulses. Strike a gong; twirl a prayer wheel, somebody's soul needs saving.

Here's the offer: I will hold the door open for all card-shark Monks to enter the promised land before I step through. All I ask for is endless cups of Yak-butter tea.

Card Playing Monks
Getting to Xiahe can be dangerous. Make sure you take the official bus. All the mini buses are staffed with gangs of thugs, who charge you double or only take you part way. On our bus they threatened to throw some fellow passengers and their luggage off the cliff. Luckily we were able to bluff them with evil eye stares and lots of shouting.

Geraldo and the Surfing Buddhas

Geraldo! Nothing makes you feel more crab apple pie, more movie stars and stripes, more guns are rights, more football hut-hut-hut, more sixties acid wash, more cherry- popping tree, more lightbulb-computor-big time wrestling get out of my way I'm trying to drive, more hours of endless television than Geraldo. This affect is increased tenfold when the sighting is in China.

One minute I was marveling at the Incredible Army of Terra Cotta Warriors and the next I'm shaking hands with Mr. Geraldo Rivera, traveling with his own camera crew to ask the American people on holiday what they thought of Clinton's visit to the middle kingdom. Wow; Mao! It's Geraldo!

So I tell him about the Surfing Buddhas. Being cool, he asks me what kind of boards they use. At first I didn't hear him, so I said, "What?" He repeats himself. It was one of those awkward celebrity meeting moments when you are trying to be breezy and light but you keep saying, "What? What did you say?" knowing you are blowing it.

Knowing this is your chance to become the first poet to write for a network sleaze show. Knowing it won't happen because you can't understand his perfect television accent. You are staring at his mustache and finally he says, "You know, long boards or short boards, what do they ride?" "They don't ride no boards, they ride crabs, mules, dolphins, flowers, cats, dogs, birds, fish. They surf the huge wave walls of the Bamboo Temple. Carved 100 years ago. After the sculptor finished, he disappeared, mysterious, gone! One Buddha has a twenty foot long arm, another Buddha has three foot long eyebrows, otherwise they are very life-like, so much so that shivers run up your soul from all of them looking at you. I mean there you are enjoying yourself like at any art attraction, when you feel as if you are being watched by some guy with an eye in his forehead or someone with his head opening up like a zipper with another head hatching out! There are about a hundred of these surfing Buddhas each as real as a face on the street, each with glass eyes that reflect your thoughts, each happy to be surfing, happy to be Buddha, frozen in this moment of joyous repose!" I'm speaking extremely fast, thinking this is very cool, and hoping Geraldo is thinking I must be cool too.

Even if you hate Geraldo, you would have to admit that the real Geraldo, not the tiny electric TV image but the in the flesh Rolling Stone kissing Geraldo is mighty mighty. I'm feeling damn patriotic when he lights up the camera and asks what I think of Clinton visiting China and say, "The further away from Washington he is, the better he looks." Then I remember a news talk show from the day before and start to quote from it as if I could really think of something like, "China has made a lot of progress but there needs to be more." Geraldo smells a rat and ends the interview saying I sound like a politician. Which I know means don't call us, we'll call you. I know I won't make it on the "Good Morning America" show and be discovered and become a TV poet guy.

Later I think I should have said, "Sheriff Starr and the Republican posse may think Washington isn't big enough for them and Clinton, but the American people love our sax playing, dope smoking, cigar-pussy licking Pres. You are making it seem like we are obsessed with sex. Which we are, but why let everyone know? Besides the scandal is lowering our exchange rate around the world, so kiss my liberal hole you big self righteous bullies!"

But that was hours after Geraldo had left town himself. That is my life; always thinking of what to say after, never during, which is what they must mean when they say, "Live in the moment." Which sounds good, but what does it mean?

There was the episode earlier when I said, "I don't know what is more exciting, the Terra Cotta mudmen or Geraldo Rivera," to which he turned and smiled his 100 watt empty-vault smile. Now that is something to make you stand up and put your hand on your heart and say, "I pledge allegiance to this guy." Something in the moment American.

Song of the Bound Feet

Hammered rice
singing.

Each bowl
a field of
green
tears.

Cracking
with any
step.

Beautiful
tea cups
caged.

Song of the Bound Feet
This poem is based on an instrumental music piece from the Tang Dynasty. Performed by the
Naxi Music Orchestra in Lijiang. It is inspired by an old Chinese saying about the toil it takes
for the harvest of the rice crop. Today the farmers thresh their grain by laying the stalks across
the road and letting the passing buses and cars crush them.

Teahouse Rappers

The Teahouse is as small as Tiananmen Square is giant. Its place in the world holds an opposite weight. Where the square, gate, buildings and Mao's huge hanging face say "I will conquer the world," the Teahouse's hot smoky blank walls are a crib giving rebirth to the freedom of the old voice of laughter, of thought. Mao lying in the soft light of god-sleep is within walking distance should he ever get thirsty or want company. I know they would pour him endless hot water and he would find the China he was afraid of; smart, funny, happy China. The little Teahouse is down an alley in the old market, just past the public toilet reeking of night soil. Before we get to hear the rap we've come for we must listen to 3 hours of stories and jokes in Mandarin plus drink hundreds of cups of tea. While we wait and drink, let me tell you two stories of poetry in China.

"Use wire, see his skin is darker than ours, hang him! Hang him!"

Thus begins a short story by Xuan Ke, recounting an incident from his 21 years in jail during the Cultural Revolution. When I met him he rolled up his sleeves and revealed the thick black scars above his wrists burned into his skin from his torture.

"This meant I was strong, tougher than the Han was. Two men rushed to the factory for tools to hack the wire to make it sharp. I had been hung 50 times before, with rope but never with wire."

Xuan Ke was jailed for his knowledge and ability as a poet, musician, and artist and because he couldn't keep his thoughts to himself. Jailed because he talked too much. Today he is free and he can't stop talking. His favorite English phrase is "Why not?"

Xuan Ke goes crazy when he thinks of Karaoke music, he is sure it is the ruin of all music and civilization of the world. I enlisted in his Anti-Karaoke Army. In China, you do what you can. Perhaps you cannot speak out against the government, but you certainly don't have to put up with canned bouncing ball ballads or the vacant sing-along images.

The Cultural Revolution is over, aren't things different now? Well yes, in many ways China has changed and there is more freedom. However in February of 1998 four poets were arrested. Their names are Wu Rouhai, Xiong Jinren, Ma Zhe, and Ma

Death to Karaoke! — Gary and Xuan Ke

Quiang. They were put in jail for planning a literary journal. Public performances seem to be o.k. but publishing is still risky. A few months later their friend was arrested for leaking to the press information of the poets' arrest. This is how much Beijing fears poetry, fears freedom of thought, and still controls the flow of information.

Pray for them. Write them a poem. Send a letter, an e-mail, light a candle say their names, "Wu, Xiong, Ma and Ma." Remember how lucky you are the next time you go to a reading and hear some suck-bottom-poet read his oh-me-oh-my bull-hooey. In China, they put the good ones away for safekeeping.

Now we are back at the Teahouse on cup 99 of extra-dose-caffeine tea listening to Mandarin for hours, which must be something like how a dog feels. You know people are good and they will feed you but what the "woof" are they talking about?

The Teahouse Rappers, or as they call themselves, Cross Talkers, were funny and entertaining. They were insulting each other in a playful way. They wore long robes with high-buttoned necks giving the appearance of the old China they were recreating. During one act performed by two boys around the age of 10, one mimed speech while the other hid behind him and sang/spoke in a wiry high voice. Then the star of the show, a young guy of about 20 brought out the clappers, similar to castanets and started clacking them and rapping. The crowd went wild. Well, they stopped drinking tea for a moment and clapped along with one hand.

So bursting with liquid we wandered back down to T-Square with its empty lap of concrete. The Chinese and American flags limp, almost touching. Sometime earlier or later, I can't remember which, President Clinton limo'd by in his motorcade waving his lonely wave.

Tea
The tea houses in China are great hang out spots. Long suppressed under Communists rule they are once again flourishing.

Xuan Ke

From the rafters, by his wrists he was hung.
In his laughter, the sound of jail.
The wire cutting English from his tongue.

His crime; foreign language poetry sung.
Come into the camp of learning and fail.
From the sun, on dark wires he was hung.

Sing the rice straight; for hours he swung.
He hides behind his hand, fingers a veil.
The wire cutting English from his tongue.

His teeth are cracked, how he comes unstrung.
He laughs, he whispers revolution's tale.
Passing out, by his pain, still he hung.

He fills your ears with bells of scars unsung.
In a small cricket cage, a nightingale.
The wire cutting English away from his tongue.

He talks too much, his words swollen and stung.
Repeat after him: shake loose one story of hell.
Mr. China's Son; by his wrists he was hung.
The wire cutting English quick from his tongue.

Xuan Ke
Is the leader of the Naxi Music Orchestra in Lijiang, China. He spent 21 years in jail during the Cultural Revolution. Each night at the orchestras performances he would rant against Karaoke music. All the concert goers complained he talked too much, still his passion was infectious. In person he always spoke in a whisper and made sure that no one was around who spoke English when he talked of his torture and his time in jail.

The Road

Zhang Yang Hao

Translated by Xaun Ke and Gary Mex Glazner

> The mountain peaks are gathering.
> The waves of the yellow river boil.
> Tong Guan road snakes
> between mountain and river.
> I look back over my shoulder
> to the ancient capital.
> I see the ghosts of the warriors.
> My heart is captured.
> Palaces and homes turn to mud.
> A country raised on the
> bitter backs of the people.
> A country falls
> with their sharp tears.

Zhang Yang Hao, *Yuan Dynasty (1270-1329)*
In Jinan, you can visit the Lingyan Temple. There you will find the "Tortoise Stone," with this inscription: "The stone was left behind in Yun Zhuang, the villa of the famous poet Zhang Yang-Hao of the Yuan Dynasty. The stone is about 4 meters high, 8 tons in weight. It is delicate, bright and is one of the four magic stones besides Dragon, Phoenix and Unicorn. It is the most famous stone in Jinan." This poem is one of Xuan Ke's favorites. Even though it speaks of a time far removed, it captures his view of the Communist regime.

Waves Washing the Sands

Li Yü

translation Xuan Ke and Gary Mex Glazner

Before the bamboo curtain.
The beating sound of rain.
It is springtime.
Where is spring's green smell?
Even a king's quilt of silk
cannot keep me warm.
Sleeping comes the dream
I am not in prison.
I wake up very late again.

Don't look out of the balcony.
Mine was a beautiful kingdom.
An endless world.
To say goodbye is easy.
To see it is impossible.
On the stream float
petals of flowers.
Now spring is gone.
Above is the sky.
Below is the earth.

Li Yü (*937-978*)

On his 41st birthday the Sung emperor sent him a gift of poisoned wine. See the book *The Silk Dragon*, translations by Arthur Sze for more poems by classic and modern Chinese poets. Working on translations with Xuan Ke was one of the highlights of the trip. He had good, but rudimentary English skills. He would tell me the story of the poem, I would write it out, and then we would go back and forth in an exchange until the poem worked for both of us.

Jade Dragon Snow Mountain

Yang Ming Yi signs his poems, "An old boy of seventy-eight." He writes in three languages; Chinese, English, and Naxi. Written, Naxi is a system of pictographs or pictograms. The symbols are representational. Used primarily to record myths, legends, and religious beliefs. Yang is unique in using the pictograms for poetry. Here is an example of one of his poems, followed by his translation:

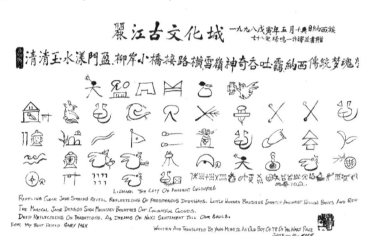

Lijaing: City of Ancient Cultures

Rippling clear jade streams
revel reflections
of prosperous doorways.
Little wooden bridges
stretch amongst
willow banks
and roads.
The magical
Jade Dragon Snow Mountain
breathes out colorful clouds.
Naxi dreams
fill our souls.

Gary and Yang

Yang's house is off the main square in the old part of Lijiang. He hangs his poems on his door. This brings him visitors from around the world. He brings out a box, "This box is all my friends from Australia." The box is crammed with letters, post cards, and trinkets. He brings out another box, "These are from my friends in Canada." He has more than twenty boxes.

Descended from the Tibetans, the Naxi are a matrilineal society. The older women wear a costume consisting of a blue smock which they wear underneath a skin of goat fur and a cape adorned with stars and moons. Peter Goullart describes Lijiang around 1940:

" Unmarried girls, locally called pangchinmei, in their best dresses and adornments, walked arm and arm in rows of four or five girls, just wide enough to block the street. In this way they charged up and down the street, giggling, singing and cracking their sunflower seeds. The unwary young man was soon engulfed by these amazons and led away to an unknown fate. The more sophisticated boys lined the walls and doors of the shops and made comments on the marching beauties. From time to time a group of girls paused before one of them, there was a scuffle, a brief and ineffectual struggle, and he was led, imprisoned in the ring of giggling and screaming furies, the destination for these prisoners, probably only too willing, was the park where dancing continued till midnight on the meadows by the river around the brightly burning bonfire."

Now the center of Lijiang is full of shops geared for tourists, but turn off of one of the main streets and you will be rewarded with old stone buildings and stone streets slick with years of walking, and a glimpse of ancient China. It is in this setting that we saw *Titanic*, dubbed into Chinese. The voice-over actors were more dramatic than the English speaking stars.

Lijiang revels in the past and the present. Yang Ming Yi's poems are a perfect mixture and reflection of that state with the Naxi, Chinese and English co-existing on the same page. Created by his hand and shared with countless visitors. Sit with him on his courtyard, drink hot tea. Give him a poem or a picture, let him file you away into the appropriate box so you may be remembered under the Jade Dragon Snow Mountain.

How the English Bury Poets

You must be dead, except for Robert Graves who was alive at the time of his being memorialized among the poets of the First World War in the Poet's Corner of Westminster Abbey. "My subject is war and the pity of war and the poetry is in the pity." When asked if he minded, he replied, that he would rather like to attend his own memorial service.

It all started with Chaucer. The first poet buried in the Poet's Corner, it is unlikely his burial in Westminster Abbey was because of his verse. Chaucer lived near the church and was at one time the Clerk of the King's works at Westminster; this was his ticket in.

Spencer was poet number two in the greatest-hits bone yard of poesy. His service was attended by all the bards of his time including, legend has it, Shakespeare. At the end of his service they are said to have each tossed in a poem and their quills to honor their friend. Ever since, they have piled on the poets.

Lewis Carrol's memorial reads, " Is all our life but a dream?" Poet's Corner seems a bit of a dream when you enter. The Corner is lit by a large rose window. An old uncle's attic stuffed with statues and carvings. Crowded and cramped, the floors and walls are dense with homage. Having run out of room, the memorials will now extend to names inscribed on the stained glass windows. Beneath it, in the angles above the right and left arches, are two carvings depicting angels or they could be winged muses.

It took all the poets in a gang to equal Shakespeare's grave and the powers of authority wanted to move him to Westminster but perhaps were stopped by this inscription on his grave.

> "Good friend for Jesus sake forbeare
> To digg the dust enclosed heare;
> Blese be man yt spares these stones
> And curst be he yt moves my bones"

Was it Shakespeare who wrote these lines? Tradition has it he wrote the passage to ensure his remains would rest undisturbed, as the custom was to remove them to the near by bone-house after a period of time. He's buried in his hometown of Strafford-upon-Avon. His birth house is intact as is the school he must have attended.

Both draw you to the question. Could anyone have known his genius, how he would come to be regarded? The house he lived in as an adult was destroyed, partly because the owner was tired of people coming by asking if Shakespeare had lived there.

Many of the main streets in Strafford retain their names and the general shape from Shakespeare's day. Floating down the river behind the church where he is buried it is not hard to drift back to those times. Stroll over to Anne Hathaway's thatched cottage with bushy garden, listen to the birds and perhaps the faint echo of young Will asking for her hand. While Strafford retains its small village charm, back at the Abbey, London crackles with the energy of the future. Before we go back to the city lets hear Shakespeare's "Sonnet 71":

> No longer mourn for me when I am dead
> Than you shall hear the surly sullen bell
> Give warning to the world that I am fled
> From this vile world with vilest worms to dwell;
> Nay, if you read this line, remember not
> The hand that writ it, for I love you so
> That I in your sweet thoughts would be forgot,
> If thinking on me then should make you woe.
> O if I say you look upon this verse,
> When I perhaps compounded am with clay,
> Do not so much as my poor name rehearse,
> But let your love even with my life decay,
> Lest the wise world should look into your moan,
> And mock you with me after I am gone.

Westminster Abbey is set in the heart of London. Big Ben chimes down the street. There is an unmistakable vitality today. The black cabs are spotlessly clean and you feel like you are riding in a 30's gangster limousine. The red phone booth boxes bristle with flyers displaying the latest spanking-caining-disipline ads. Big hatted Bobbies happily twirl their batons. Most amazing of all, the food is good; from Indian to Pub Grub the sun never sets hungry. With the pound strong, it is no wonder that many foreign poets are dying to get into the Abbey.

Longfellow is the only American. T.S. Elliot and Henry James started their lives as Yanks and became permanent ex-patriots. Is there evidence that their naturalization was an attempt to increase their chances of being memorialized in the Poet's Corner?

Gerard Manley Hopkins' memorial reads, "Immortal Diamond," although "Immortal Diamond spot-on," would be springier.

Dylan Thomas', that brilliant downer of liquids, says, "Time held me green and dying. Though I sang in my dream like the sea."

Auden's replies, "In the prison of his days, teach the free man to praise."

"O Rare Ben Johnson," has a handsome bust and may be the only poet who is buried standing up.

Robert Browning was living with Elizabeth Barret in Venice at the time of his death. His body was brought to the Abbey. How do I bury thee? Let me count the ways.

Matthew Arnold saw death this way, "Let but the light appear and the transfigured wall be touch'd with flame."

Since Byron waited 145 years for his memorial, the lines "But there is that within me which shall tire/ torturous amid time and breath when I expire," are especially poignant. His body taken to England after his death in Greece was refused burial in Westminster Abbey. He was buried with his family near Newstead. Three requests for his memorial had been turned down. The last unsuccessful attempt was in 1924, when the Dean of the day, Bishop Herbert E. Ryle wrote:

> "Byron, partly by his own openly dissolute life and partly by the influence of licentious verse, earned a worldwide reputation for immorality among English-speaking people. A man who outraged the laws of our Divine Lord, and whose treatment of women violated the Christian principles of purity and honor, should not be commemorated in Westminster Abbey."

In the wild sixties, Byron was forgiven and his spirit reunited with Keats, and Shelly, whose names are set together in twin oval tablets. Tainted with Shelly's atheism they had only been memorialized in 1954.

While I was having a moment with Milton, I overheard a workman say to a priest, "Let's just put it this way, there are some people who get away with murder." What he was referring to I have no idea, but with centuries of dead gathered round, killing was in the air.

At night, all the bones rattle and the poets come out. Who is the greatest? Who is the prettiest? Buried together, memorialized together, never wanting for company, the only problem is everyone else is a poet too. Perhaps they would rather be alone, instead of listening to the nightly call of the history of English poetry.

I know what you are thinking, "How can I get into Poet's Corner?" So I wrote the Abbey and asked how someone is chosen to be memorialized there. Here is the answer from the holy press agent.

Dear Gary,
Thank you for your email. Poets are selected firstly by their name being
put forward and then our Dean and Chapter, after great deliberation, are the
ones who decide.

Take care,
Jackie Pope

Well that seems easy enough, just get your friends to send in a collection plate full of requests, then donate a godly sum of money for new choir robes, button-hole the Dean over sacramental wine, break bread with the Chapter and you're in. Oh, one more thing, it wouldn't hurt to write several hundred sonnets or have plays that are still staged 400 years after your death. Lets face it, unless they open a web-sight version, your chances and mine are about as good as Mrs. Amanda McKittrick Ros, a writer with a gift for, as she puts it, "disturbing the bowels."

Ros blazed the metaphor trail with; "globes of glare" (eyes) and "globules of liquid lava" (sweat). In her poem, "On Visiting Westminster Abbey", she states, "A reduced dignity invited me to muse on its merits." Capturing the feelings of countless poets, "How can it be complete if I'm not there?"

Doors

You must answer
this question first,
exterior or interior?

To hang the door
never use gravity.

Hinges are flapping
metal wings.
Miter them a nest.

Door to Mr. Shakespeare's grave

Wait for light
to shine a path,
seal off the glow.

Chisel away any
surface that slows
your step.

Let it swing, see how
it rides, this moment
of entrance.

Misalign? Springs open?
Sticks? Rattles?
Look into your tool box,
speak with the muse,
slip in the key.

Confess.
Step through,
disappear.

Tea

Steam is the first sip
touch air with taste.

Scent is the second sip
tang of union.

Too hot, hint of purity,
lips recoil.
Now the waiting,
place hands
on edge of vessel.
Listen for cooling.

No one knows where the drink
comes from,
it shows up in the kitchen
a guest.
Be a good host, ask the kettle
why it sings.

Caress the handle with flesh.
Open your mouth to its mouth.
Inhale the last drop of coming honey.
What pleasure the empty cup
knows.

On the Bus

"Why do you shoot rockets?"

The question sears the air. A moment before we had been refreshing ourselves with lemon scented oil. Poured by the bus attendant, the fragrance helped the passengers cool off, helped relieve the monotony of the long hours of slow cross country travel. We were on the bus from Istanbul to Ephesus, anonymous travelers now called to explain our position as Americans. We Americans had just bombed Afghanistan and the Sudan in retaliation for the attacks on the embassies in Africa. I could tell them the official line, that we were targeting the terrorists we believed were responsible for the deaths in the embassies or I could say how some people believed it was to distract the media attention from Clinton's affair with Monica. I could bring up the fact that as an average citizen, I really had no control over our government, how I too felt helpless in the face of such events. Perhaps I should use the occasion to bring up how much good America does, with relief efforts and foreign aid. I could cry out but I am a poet, traveling around the world trying to understand your culture, any culture. We could talk about how the United States doesn't even really have a culture, unless you count big haired rockers and aren't they really from England anyway? This would be the perfect moment to talk about freedom and face veils for women. They would retort, "What about the veil you hide behind? Your arrogant imperialistic world view! You look down on everyone don't you?"

The question filled the bus with tension. My mind was whirling with the possible out-come of a bad answer. I was thinking about the oppressions of the regime in Turkey, how they jailed writers who spoke out for religious freedoms. In this case the freedom for the conservative faction of Muslims. A bizarre twist to the freedom of speech calls from left wing radicals in the United States. Here was a country that saw the need to imprison people in order to keep their secular government, to keep it free from the radical religion. How did our rockets fit into this world view?

Then an old man smiled and gave the thumbs-up, universal sign for kick-ass. Then another passenger mimed a machinegun, making rapid fire bullet sounds. The bus filled with fake gun and bomb sounds; an imaginary battle ground of Turkish warriors. Force was something we all could understand. Amid the pow-pow-pow and bang-bang you're dead we all could feel the helplessness of being ordinary citizens. This play acting bridged our language gap. Let us be together as people. For a moment our only worry is getting more lemon-scented oil.

CUMALI KIZIK

Water Prayer

Water comes down
the village stones,
gleaming, washing,
cold. Filling the
streets with
wet life, cobble
soaked, flowing.
Flowers reflect
the walls,
mustard, berry, sky.
Men
shoe a horse. A dog
growls, barks.
Watermelons
cool in the
fountain.
Two girls are
sketching,
the buildings,
with soft
gray lines.
Does the air
stop at the door
with a loud blue knock?
What fish swim
here when it rains?
Where does the river walk?
Who thought
to scrub the
lanes with a
smell as clear
as prayer?

The Mystic Barber of Selçuk

Like other men of a certain age, I am becoming concerned with my place in the world and what to do with excess ear hair. It was towards the end of my first Turkish haircut that I became aware it might hold the answers to both these questions.

My wife and I were in the small town of Selçuk on the west coast of Turkey. We had toured the impressively restored ruins of Ephesus, outside of town, and now we were ready to relax.

As we passed a barbershop, I saw that one of the chairs was empty. Impulsively feeling in need of a little Turkish trim, I stuck my head in the doorway. A teenager motioned me to sit down. I was surprised to find that he was the barber, and that the seven-year-old with him was his assistant.

For a while everything went according to plan, even with the language difficulties. When called upon, I would make the appropriate motion for "short" or the buzzing sound of the razor clippers. I thought we were close to being done when suddenly the haircut took off like the first drop of a roller-coaster. My stomach flew into my throat, and in an instant I was out of my seat yelping, my arms flailing. The assistant had stuck a ball of flame into my ear.

I had seen it out of the corner of my eye: a ball of cotton on a stick, a giant Q-tip. The seven-year-old had dipped it in a liquid, then with the flick of a lighter, the cotton burst into flame. It briefly dawned on me that this action was part of the Turkish haircut ritual, a big change from the hunting-fishing-sports talk that define the American male clip-bonding experience. Then he plunged in the tiki-torch and I smelt the stink of burning hair. My hair.

That's when I leapt out of the chair. But after many assurances that innumerable customers before me had all undergone this same treatment without suffering noticeable scars or sears, I reluctantly returned to the seat.

The torching passed with just the barest of burning sensations, then the barber took two thin strings and began flossing my face, eliminating any fuzz from my cheeks. Next he filled his hands with a lemon-scented oil and clamped down on my nose until I gasped for breath.

As I started to hyperventilate, I realized that this would be a great technique for the "Panting Dervish" — a lesser-known sect similar to the poet Rumi's "Whirling Dervish," who go into a trance to get closer to God, not by spinning but by heavy breathing. We had seen the whirling dervishes perform their ritual in Istanbul a few days before; now the men and women in their brightly colored robes turned and turned in my mind.

Then I had an image of Rumi. The story goes that he started his whirling dervish dance while walking and hearing the musical hammering of a goldsmith. As he listened to the pounding of the hammer on metal, he began to rotate. As the pounding quickened, he went into a spin, growing dizzy and entering a trance, feeling God.

I never quite understood the reason he started to spin, but now I knew the missing part of the story. He spun because he was having a haircut and his ears were blazing! Rushing out of the barbershop, Rumi knew if he didn't do something drastic he would fry to a crisp. So around in circles the master went until the fire was out.

When your ear is being flambéed, you are closer to God, going into a trance, leaping and spinning like a dervish to extinguish the flame. You see things. You know what Rumi means when he says, "The light you give off did not come from a pelvis." No, it came from an ear!

I panted and jerked, providing great entertainment for the gang in the barber shop. Then the tonsorial teen pushed my head down into the sink, soaking me with ice cold water. He began to massage my neck, pulled me up in my seat and nuzzled me. I can't remember the last time a barber nuzzled me. Jerking my head back and forth, he attempted to pop the bones in my neck. When that didn't work, he switched to karate chops, ending with a very traditional blow dry and the spraying of a manly cologne.

As my time in the mystic-barber's chair came to an end, I knew the most efficient technique for the removal of unwanted hair follicles: use fire. As for my place in the world, I keep thinking about those large chunks of skewered turning meat you see all over Turkey.

The Mystic Barber of Selçuk
The ruins of Ephesus feature marble roads with chariot ruts, public baths, and a carved sign for the corner brothel. Ephesus was the sight of a huge temple to worship the goddess Artemis and not coincidentally later sanctified as the final home of Mary, Mother of Jesus.

Delphic Oracle

The Oracle is gone.
She has left the rocks as prophets.

They know the yellow
of the sun's sour heat. What trees drink.

The immovable rocks are spewing forth
their nonsense; I'll interpret.

They are disgusted by the lack of air.
They await the rebirth of breath.

Sounding voices
of the nations of the world.

They understand every tongue.
They speak the silence between languages.

Sweeping away the dirt from your grave,
I touch the granite above your bones.

In the valley of Delphi,
you came back to die.

You loved the fabric of this land.
Wove your own cloth
of light and myth.

You are not the Oracle,
although your seed
is buried with her.

I have so many questions,
if I started to ask, I would
also lie down forever.

Live as these rocks live.
    See the future they see.

Calling all oracles!

The Oracle of Delphi
Angelos Sikelianos is one of Greece's best-loved modern poets. In the 1920's Angelos and Eva
Sikelianos recreated the Delphi Games, including performances of dance and poetry. Eva wove
the costumes. I refer to her at the end of the poem. The prophecies of the Oracle were transmit-
ted as poetry. Angelo's great-granddaughter is the American poet, Eleni Sikelianos.

Wedding Dance

Greeting us at the port on the Greek island of Naxos is a large open doorway, to an unfinished temple. We enter the island through this frame. Watching the sea come yellow, orange, then fading blue-black. Walking into town we reach a church. The chapel is dressed in white and the scent of anise. Families fill the courtyard. A string of clear light bulbs drape off the bell tower to the ground. Entering the church, all the people are talking, laughing with old friends, family, flirting. A hunched over woman in black weaves through the crowd lighting candles. Children play. The priest is blessing the young couple on the altar; a man off to the side begins to sing. The wedding dance. The guests as flock of birds, turn and soar, throw rice, never asking why this ritual. The priest and wedding party circle the altar, small steps. The crowd responds, air white with rice. The friends of the bride and groom zinging rice. The priest ducks behind an icon using the painted board as his shield. Grains fill hair and clothes. The priest peeks out. Hit, he takes cover again. Crazy rice, unquestioning rice, wild party, a million white wiggling tails. The bride's mother races to protect her daughter's veil; she takes the bullet, caught in a crossfire. The barrage winds down, a toss, a last flick. They are dignity; ready for new voices, new words, fertilized with magic and grain they may now face all onslaught.

.

Wedding Dance
Naxos is famous for its sweet lemon liquor, we would drink it after midnight with barbecued octopus.

Sandal Maker Poet

The sign says "Poet." In the plaza below the Acropolis on a narrow street lined with tourist traps there is a shop outside of which the owner has hung his declaration. Inside you find Stavros Melissinos, Sandal Maker Poet. Face and hands worn and cracked. When I ask him to read me one of his poems he asks, "In Greek?" Moves close, whispering. As he recites, I imagine the words to be anything. The most fascinating poem ever written:

"Take away the glories
and the honors
the granite palace
of this vain world
and only give me
the smile of pain,
the tear of joy. and
I will erect
a thousand palaces in me
in which to live."

He knows something gets lost and says, "Translations, ahhhhh!" Melissinos oils his leather skins. His shop is cluttered with sandals hanging from the low ceiling, covering the walls. He believes that making things with his hands helps his poetry, that working with your hands gives you a subject. When we leave he puts a chair in the doorway with a closed sign. Sitting down he begins to write. The poet is open.

Sandal Maker Poet
Melissinos had sold sandals to everyone from the Beatles to Sophia Loren. When his children asked why he didn't get the Beatles' autographs, he said, "Why should I? They come to see me."

Knossos Cicadas

Whistle your
bones. Wail,
strings of harp.

Hear this
song calling
to the ground,
to crumble.

Sing to dust,
to stone.

Salt into
earth.

Live with the
shells of your
voices.

Cease.

Finding Mario

His poster was on the door of a delicatessen, announcing a new book of poems. "¿Donde esta Mario?" I said in Spanish to the Italian shopkeeper. She took me onto the street and pointed, "Take the first alley on the left, then the first door; that's Mario." Seconds later I was pressing his buzzer. A minute later a head poked out of the window.

"Hello," I said, "Do you speak English?"

"No," he replied.

"Me parlo Italian un poco." I was sharp with my mixture of English, bad Spanish and worse Italian.

"Are you Mario Stefano?"

"No." He came back quickly. He looked like the guy on the flyer. With the narrow alley, I was looking straight up so it was hard to tell for sure.

"Are you the poet Mario Stefano?"

"No."

Again no, I was stunned. I was sure I had the right door.

"Do you have a new book of poetry?"

"Yes."

Now we were getting somewhere.

Very slowly, I pronounced every letter of his name as if by slowing my speech he would suddenly remember he was the famous poet, M-a-r-i-o S-t-e-f-a-n-o "NO!"

He disappeared back into the building

I rang the bell again. He thrust his head out of the window.
"Do you have a book of poetry?"
"Yes"
"But you are not Mario Stefano the poet?"
"NO, MARIO STEFANI!"
Then he was gone again.

Drinking
MARIO STEFANI

We drink on Monday.
We drink on Tuesday.
We drink on Wednesday.
We're running out of days to drink

Nubian Insect Poet in Tuscany

Nubian Insect Poet in Tuscany
with his wife of 22 years, Fioralla Rossi

He buzzes and folds his hands
as if in prayer. He bows his head,
then looks up at me. Mamdoh has
turned into a Ladybug. Flitting and
buzzing he has a door, not a macho
door with fire and a guard, just a
little door with small birds on the
steps. To go through his door you must
walk gently and carefully. He says
everyone has a door. There are billions
of doors in the world. Maybe his door
is not for everyone. He says he likes
the American poet Walt Whitman, and
Whitman has a door.
I tell him Whitman has a big door
and a window.

Mamdoh Badran

Mamdoh Badran is an amazing painter. He brings the wonderful light of Tuscany alive in his watercolors. He gave me a tape recording of his Nubian poetry with harp accompaniment. The language was dark, a humming, throbbing of wings. This ancient language brought to him by parental ghosts, the spirit of poetry transmitted by insects, the light of Tuscany in his brush. Mamdoh smiled, and said, "Too much English, it makes my head hurt." I imagine conversing, in Italian, Nubian, Ladybug and English, with different species and voices from the beyond could very well bring on a migraine.

Dinner Last Night

Game stew; a creamy bowl of mushrooms with chunks of soft tender venison. Steaming broth of delightful flavor overlooking Budapest, the lights, flickering eat me. Mushrooms in a pastry shell with a kiwi garnish. Protecting and cuddling the mushrooms. Entrée: fillet of pork smothered in mozzarella cheese with a hint of basil surrounded by piles of french fries cut lean and tender. The lights singing a melody of "Like a Virgin and Don't Cry for Me Argentina." Beverage: a cold frothy beer in a tall narrow glass. Impeccable service, swift and decisive like the threat of a samurai's sword. I bite, chew, swallow and stagger back up the hill to the Citadel and our wonderful room full of pigeon feathers and falling plaster. A huge room with beds for five and lockers for thirty and sheets which do not cover the mattress. The next morning, my bag was stolen at the train station. Later that day, I noticed an abcess on my gums that required immediate dental surgery and an eight day stay in Prague. I'll always remember that dinner. Food as a map.

Vienna
We only stayed in Austria for half a day, it was cold, wet and no one was waltzing.

Margaret in Budapest on Margaret Street. Poets like this sort of serendipity, synchronicity, and the simultaneous (as well as the sibilant sonority of alliteration).

The Poetry Jazz Cave

The room is packed with ex-pat poets, boho Czechs, frothy big beers and Kafka's ugly cousins. You're wondering about Prague. Reading about the hipness in your Sunday newspaper. You've heard about the invasion of intellectual-artist-writer babes and boys. Heard about the cheep beer, pink tanks and piles of fried, almost-for-free meat meals. Have you ever thought of making the scene, breaking free from big-daddy-mommy America? Learning some scary language words. Changing the brand of cigs you smoke to something foreign and strong? Do you ever wonder what Paris was like for Hem, Gurdie, and Fitz? What the Village was like for young Kerouac? What the Beats knew about fresh brew in North Beach? Of course you have. Then the Jazz Poetry Cave is your happening Johnny-on-the-pony, right now, right on, get down gig.

So step down, put your name on the list and get ready to poetry and roll. First, argue with the doorman. Surely he don't want no Kroners if you are poet.

Look it's Magic Larry, the old hippie bard who runs the Jazz Cave Poetry Jam. Better chat with him if you're gonna read. Everybody is already gathered; Paul Polansky, the boxer poet who uncovered the Gypsy concentration camp Letty, Gwen Albert and Mr. Farnsworth who run the crazy zine JeJune, Theo with his dog Basket and head full of psychedelic rap sonnets and dozens of other muse seekers. Here's an open seat, squeeze in and order a round.

The band is warming up; nose rings and tattoos vibrating. Rakish tie-dyes hanging off their skinny bodies. Before we get started, one of

Paul Polansky in Prague.

the women musicians has an announcement, first in English then Czech. "I have been asked by the other members of the band to bring my baby to this Poetry Jam Jazz Cave. As you can see, the cave does not have much ventilation. I ask you to, please, for the duration of the po-fest, to limit your smoking. If you must smoke please go out by the bar." Everyone is shocked. No one stops smoking. In the room of fifty, perhaps forty are smoking. Someone yells, "People, it is for the baby, stub your butts." A couple of people stop puffing. Some hearing the words "smoke and butts" remember that they are not smoking and light up.

The band boots into the first number. A cross between slow blues and Kenny G on speed. Magic Larry leaps onto the stage and begins to chant, "Raspberry, blueberry stirred in a pot. Mirror, mirror, who is the prettiest, who is not?" Most of the poets in the crowd take inspiration from this and begin to work on their poems, furiously scribbling, with heads down, sipping the foam from their giant pilsners. Magic L goes on, "The scum of the earth reside in the rainbow of the capitalist big-box-BOOM!" Larry's poem is grinding on ten minutes, clearly a violation of the no-time-hog poetry reading rule, as revealed by the squirming antsy pants poets. This is the moment in all poetry readings that everyone wants Shakespeare to rise again. Imagine that succulent beast coming up from the dead, shocked by the sad state of the sonnet market. Finally, Magic Larry ends, "Trees are the souls of my roots, my boots, my scoooots." Everyone cheers. Some clearly cheering because he has finished. Like all poets he makes no judgements about applause and beams his craggy graybeard grin and announces the next reader. "Ladies and gentlemen let's have a big Jazz Poetry Cave welcome for Paul Polansky."

Polansky is a big guy. He launches into this poem:

> After the skinheads threw
> the garbage cans
> through our window,
> we moved out of Prague.
>
> We bought a shack
> in the country,
> acquired a watch dog,
> and surrounded ourselves
> with barbed-wire.

But I know
we will never have peace
until I dye
my children's hair blond
and buy a drug to change
the color of their skin.

I've promised my sons
when I get some money
that's what I'm going to do
for them.

Gwen Albert leans over and whispers, "That's Polansky's poem, 'A Sinti Mother Speaks,' from his book *Living Through it Twice*. Polansky writes in the voices of Czech Roma he met during his research of the World War II death camp at Lety, outside of Prague. He was doing research on immigration from Czechoslovakia to the United States, at the Trebon State Archive, when he came across the documents of the concentration camp for the Roma. They told him that no survivors existed, but through his own research he was able to track down over sixty of them." The images hang in the air haunting us.

Next up is the hunch back, Rastafarian, dwarf, illegitimate love child of Vaclav Havel, Frank Zappa and Madeleine Albright. He breaks into a language/concrete poem that consists of chewing a large chunk of styrofoam and whispering in villanelle form; "Watch out where the huskies go, and don't you eat that yellow snow." During the extravaganza Gwen slips me her poem written on a napkin:

Backpack Tourist

backpack tourist radiates a searing love of horses
kindly older couples are about to take her in
nervous when the stranger drove her further
    through the
      forest
fingering the slobber on the handle of his axe

city of a hundred spires now wearing golden
arches
GYPSIES BACK TO INDI   a language no one
reads
journalists will demonstrate the need for rape and
        murder
ghosts out of the future find the service better, or?

apples pink of chalk hard of glass upon the
branches
children telling robots it's their turn to suffer eggs
barking dogs at sunset yellow leaves along the
        gutter
paradise is matter housing fire beneath the trees

A piece of the styrofoam lodges in the love child's tiny throat. Mr. Farnsworth rushes to the stage and while performing the Heimlich Maneuver begins a lecture on the moral instruction of didactic verse and I mean didactic in the most gentle and pure sense.

He recites this poem as an illustration of his poetic belief system.

(not long) after Creeley

the palms were slaughtered

everyone turned into animals
and jumped overboard
washed up and dug holes in the sand
that continue to fill with water and we
bailed buckets of fish schematics
and globs of loaves,

descended the here of the hole
filling with the there of the sea
as found in the oxford english dictionary
some old norse link but nothing

more than the meaning which is
elementary pothead revelation,
everywhere you go there you are
yet even if you're not going anywhere
and the bud's worn off
the oscillation continues

as more pothead everywhere
in the emptying distance
everyone jumped, washed that bailed fish
scrubbed vanishing points better left unpainted
distance comparison turned overboard,
their going off continues

disoriented in the orient
dude   in a jeep
there's no front there and
what am I doing here behind enemy lines
I should be home
filling my quota of shitty things
    the ones we all got to do before coming off
    old and nice
not driving burning tires
the smell obscuring our vision
sweat of my palms on the wheel

the entire crew is slaughtered and we
continue on to the next island

The crowd rises to their feet shouting. Never have they witnessed such a combination of health care and poetical theory. Farnsworth leaps into the outstretched arms of the people and finishes his poem crowd surfing back to his seat.

Magic Larry's eyes fill with tears as he brings up the next poet. Theo has taught his dog Basket to bark in time to poems. Every fourth word is punctuated with a loud syncopated yap. Basket has a great sense of rhythm and a bushy tail. "Please people put your paws together for the next poet and his furry friend."

Theo and Basket read and howl:

The Morning I Let Nothing Go To Waste

This is the morning I let nothing go to waste
the Riesling spilled in the refrigerator
the Riesling spilled in the night
the night I did not know the eggs had spilled
the night the laundry detergent spilled in
the night all manner of things spilled repeatedly
like so many Vaclavs from so many horses.

This is the morning I let nothing go to waste
the morning I make a frittata of the eggs
the wine spilled in the eggs
the eggs of the dog that bit me
the frittata of the eggs of the dog of the wine
the tomatoes of the dog of the wine
the wine of the dog in the laundry
like so many poets from so many bridges.

This is the morning I let nothing go to waste
the morning I salvage the eggs broken
the eggs broken the broken tomatoes
the onions of the city that has no onions
the laundry detergent from the laundry room floor
the Riesling from the bottle from the saute pan
the frittata of the dog in the night
like so many Bendas from so many Bohemias.

As the reading ends, we spill out into the air, thankful to be on the Left Bank of 90's. We take a stroll across the bridge Kafka must have used to go home after a night of writing.

In the morning we all wake up to find that we have not turned into insects.

Spooning

Together chest and back, ribs to rib.
Teething the silent shadow of your hair.
You feed me the murmur of sighs.
Reach into my mouth with endless motion,
fires of absolute nourishment.
Whose skin feels this?
Twined like stems we grow into our
hearts, grow into our mysterious
banquet. Who has not fed at this table?
Honey is sour in this curving grief.
Soon the moment comes when we must break.
Fast as knives knowing we have eaten.

Spooning
Prague is a romantic city, with its old spires and bridges. It is also the capital of fried meat and
smoking. Once sitting on a bench outside in a park, we had to move because the cigarette smoke
was so thick. We rented a room in an old woman's house for 12 dollars a day. The room was full
of well tended plants. The bed covered with hand made lace.

The Learning Root

On the Church wall photos
The size and shape of apples
Hang in clustered blond rows.
Long dead angles of war.
Polished with care.
Faces coiled in smile.
Lieder song youth swallowing seeds.
Slicing blank dreams.
Bobbing for castles in the Mosel.
Whistling a planting hymn.
This is the core of civilization
Peeling away the past.
If only history were a teacher
Accepting our sweet red fruit.

The Learning Root

The old German woman rented out rooms in her house. To ascertain whether we were a couple who needed one bed or just friends travelling jointly who needed two beds, she shoved us together miming a gesture that unmistakably meant we slept with each other. We nodded yes and all laughed at this universal symbol of sex and her quick silent understanding.

Zell is famous for its Black Cat Wine. Each hotel has its own private vintage.
It has a light crisp taste with hint of forbidden fruit.

Altar

Beating black teeth—
Spell of clothes molded to honeybee bones.

All her days are the same.
A sultry gleaming skull.

Gaze begging a silent bridge.

Between devotion
       & Savior.

Feathered puppet.
   Little second coming.

Soaring machinery of blood—
      Reflection
   of fireflies.

Uttering green spin of dance.
   Initiation of the peacock's corona;
      landscape of blue chorus.

Cloak of
casket. Sweet oak
speechless.

Entering her ring.
Arcing her eager future.

Inventing her.
With words she cannot hear.

The body rhapsodic.
Nothing left but

cells
        &
                singing.*

* Who can look away?

Museum in Copenhagen
Oak Coffin found in a grave mound circa 1350. The deceased was an eighteen-year-old woman, 170 cm tall, slim with ash-blond hair with a reddish tint. Her face was long and narrow, her eyelashes long, her nose thin, her teeth large, well formed. The hair was done up into an elaborate coiffure, covered by a hairnet, She had gold rings fastened to either ear. This young woman was buried in early summer. She was dressed in a blouse with embroidery on the elbow length sleeves. A lone piece of material, gathered by a belt, covered her from the waist to the feet.

Feeling the Poem Dance

This is from an interview conducted with Bob Holman for the About.com poetry web sight on Nov. 19th, 1998, one month after the First Poetry Olympics took place in Stockholm.

Holman: Mr. Glazner sir, so good of you to be with us from your round the world perch!

Glazner: The jazz of the internet-interview is; I'm here in Barcelona accessing the electro-bits you wired from New York as questions! I'm a slow key-stroker, let me print you out so we can conduct the net-e-view at a little tapas dive just off Las Rambalas. Come on the chorizo is hot and the house red is 100 pesetas a glass, (seventy cents). Is that cowboy statue winking? He's not a statue, he wants coins! Down this narrow alley. Look up, the balconies are covered with laundry. How Gaudi. Is that the plaza? Last night it was filled with a rally. They want to extra-dite Pinochette, bring him to Spain and castrate him for the atrocities he inflicted on Spanish citizens during his reign in Chile. What fire the people have. The speaker got them chanting, they broke into a rhythmic clapping like a flamenco dance, calling out, waving "down with the devil," signs. Not your rent-a-protester tie-died whine-in like the States, but shoes-shinned middle age folks and buzz-cut college kids lisping for justice.

Here it is, "The Tapaporium." How 'bout a plate of octopus with olives? Smell the chorizo? What's this in *Time* magazine? Ted Hughes is dead. I was just reading "Birthday Letters," nice poems, but spit compared to Silvia. What really made me want to meet Hughes, sit down and share toothpicks like we're doing, was his book, *A Choice of Shakespeare's Verse*, where he stripped out sections of the plays showing how they work as poems on their own. How he ended up with two wives committing suicide, who knows? I'll miss never chatting Shakespeare with him. "Uno mas vino, por favor," this ones for Ted, but the rest of the jar is for Plath. OK lets visit the Poetry Olympics.

Holman: First, a hearty "CONGRATULATIONS!" You are the very First International Poetry Olympics Champeen. How does it feel?

Glazner: The date of the POlympics final night was October 17th 1998, eight years to the day of the First National Poetry Slam held in Frisco. I spent most of the afternoon in 1990, making the trophy, a woman's high heel boot on a stack of poetry books painted gold. So it was very sweet to receive the Swedish version, a sandal on books including sock with the paint still wet! Really, none of this poetry competition would work if the poets didn't care about winning and work on their performances. It was exciting to connect with the audience, feel the poem really dance, galloping down to the wire, nose sniffing the laurel.

Holman: What was the format in Stockholm? What teams were there?

Glazner: Bulgaria, Croatia, Estonia, Finland, Moldavia, Sweden and USA had poets represented. Only Bulgaria and Sweden had four poet teams. Same format as the slam, three-minute rule, no props, no music, except for the triathlon, which was a team, made of poet, dancer, and musician. Although since most of the poets were new to the format, we had some wonderful moments, like a poet using his shoe to represent his father, and another announcing that the poem would begin when she emerged from behind the curtain, only to disappear for a few minutes.

Holman: What languages were the poems in? Translations? What were the highlights? Did any of the poets use music or exotic performance techniques?

Glazner: The poems were mostly in Swedish and English. I was the only winner other than poets from Sweden. Poems were also read in Bulgarian, French, Moldavian, and Russian and of course, Erkki read in the language of silence. Of the translations, Moldavian into French was especially musical. One poem was read in French to the cadence of Poe´s "Raven." It was clear from the Swedes domination, that in the future having written translations into the language where the POlympics are being held would help the audience and the event.

For me, the real highlight was watching how the poet's idea of performing grew over the week. Most of the Swedish poets had been to the US Poetry Slam Nationals but for the other poets slamming was new. Their performances rapidly improved. The Bulgarians had a hilarious piece the final night that spoofed the atmosphere of the bar scene in Stockholm, with the poet being drowned out by people talking, so the poem became the background conversation. Very well done, with the poet miming on in silence.

Another highlight was the Croatian triathlon team, which was made up of a mother, son and daughter. They had a piece about leaving their country that left some of the audience in tears.

Holman: What is the future of International Slamming? Do the US Nationals relate to the Olympics at all?

Glazner: Looks like Bulgaria for next year. The POlympics is organized by the IOPP, International Organization of Performing Poets. Erkki Lappalinen is the President with Michael Brown as Secretary. So it comes right out of the National Poetry Slam, an unofficial sister thing. Next year I look for a US team chosen out of the Nationals.

Holman: Oh, and by the way, what did you win?

Glazner: 1000 Swedish Kroner, just enough to mail home the lovely golden sandal trophy.

Trophies from the Poetry Olympics.
NOTE: As of the printing of this book, the Second Poetry Olympics has yet to take place.

The Tumbleweed Hotel

Every substance has an instant just below the flash point at which any increase in temperature causes a burst of incandescence. When we travel we learn the history of fire, of places that once grew to flame. We search them out hoping a little spark will be left. A glow on which to warm our hands to feel what Rome was like. To stumble into a café and find Picasso and Apollinaire. Mostly we are groping in the dark unable to feel that heat. In Paris life is full of gorgeous flirty people, full of stunning sexy history, statues, paintings, lights, action! Still, as a newcomer you can walk for days awed by the beauty but feel the prime is gone. Paris, city of museums, keeper of relics. Hemingway once drank beer in this café. This is where Sartre and De Beauvoir huddled! Would you like a seven-dollar cup of coffee?

Then you turn into Shakespeare and Company bookstore, sitting on the bank of the Seine across from Notre Dame. George Whitman is at the helm and you are thrust into the thick of the book. The pages swirl, turn around you. Open your mouth, let the words spill. You are a character sleeping in the Tumbleweed Hotel, the rooms above the bookstore. Whitman, handsome and sharp at 84, is holding a blackened-bottom mess kit frying pan. I ask him how the Tumbleweed Hotel is doing. Sizing me up, he says,

"I can book you a room for two."

"Well we are leaving to catch a train in a few hours."

"Where are you from?"

"San Francisco."

"What is your occupation?"

"Poet."

"Then for God's sake you have to stay. We're having a pancake breakfast tomorrow morning, a tea party in the afternoon and a poet from Bengal is reading on Monday."

We stay.

Entering the room, you enter a sanctuary, books from floor to ceiling. Photos of Anais Nin, Henry Miller, Lawrence Durell, all inscribed to George. George as a young man around the blazing fire of the wishing well, where they held the readings. Grab off the shelves, a play by Picasso, *The Second Sex*, and Ginsberg's *Collected Poems* all signed. The feeling of the authors' presence is strong. They slept here, drank here, wrote here. Now it is my turn. Where are you from? Is a question we all ask. I am from Paris, but that will not last, the last free room in the world.

George is downstairs in front of the bookstore. He is dressed in coat and tie. He is from here. Opens his home like a monastery of the word. I find letters to George tucked away in books from many of the writers who have stayed here, a museum of words, a temple of language. For over 40 years, George has presided over his bookstore. It has been his passion, his view of the world. You may be asked to stay, given a room. Thousands of people have been his guests. He never asks for a penny. All he asks for is an autobiography, just a word or two about you. Wants to know where you are from. Of course sometimes he shouts at people, "Where is my damn autobiography?" or "Who left the skin on this pumpkin, I thought you said you could cook!" Once, quietly he said, "You say you are a poet but even your wife doesn't believe you."

Shakespeare and Company is a pilgrimage, a monument, each time I look out of the window someone is taking a photo of the store. They will take it back from where they are from, put it in an album and say I was there. Here, let me show you around the place. That is were Simone touched the tip of her pen to the *Second Sex*. Here is where Ginsberg clipped his beard. This refrigerator contains food made by Sylvia Beach for Pound. Now step back here. This is the bedroom so full of ghosts. The cockroach on my forehead at night was Henry Miller.

The secret to George, to the Tumbleweed Hotel, to Shakespeare and Company, is emptiness. George is empty. You must enter him. See the world through his eyes. Through his windows. He takes off his mask and there are all the faces who have stayed here. Swallowed by the stories. Why worry about myths when you can dance? Why not take his hand? It is open. Just reach out. You are common, that's reassuring. We are fallen, let us enter the door together. The gates of the bazaar. Into the word department. Let's order a full meal. Let us draw the human figure. Naked, waiting for someone to offer us love. Mischievous bookseller, who holds your council? Who have you not blessed? A sign? Of course and a caravan. Let us all pull up stakes and head off to Paris. I erect a statue in your honor. I require myself to seek out your methods, your saintliness, and your glory. Need a light?

The Tumbleweed Hotel

Staying across the river from Notre Dame for free was a dream. Each day at noon I would open the windows and give a short reading to who ever happened to be walking by. Any writer can stay, all you have to do is ask about the "Tumbleweed Hotel."

The Poetry Widow From Pomona

She's been a poetry widow for about 10 years now. Most currently in Paris. But also Stockholm, Hanoi, Kathmandu and Bangkok where she is abandoned for long periods of time so that her husband can persue his 2nd love (she knows of course that she remains his first love). and so she sits here alone once again, drafting an auto biography of sorts for Mr. George Whitman.

She was born on April 11, 1958 in Upland, California. Her parents are Becky, a homemaker and great mom, and Rex a judge. Her siblings are 4. Girls all. Elizabeth, Cathy, and the baby twins Carmen Rose and Carol Ruth. Unfortunately for Carmen and Carol she won't let them grow up even though they're in their 30s now. Always the baby sisters. And now nieces and nephews have entered the picture...6 all and a real joy.

Most of her childhood was spent in Pomona, California (hence the name poetry widow from pomona). She attended catholic schools including 4 years at the all girls school, Pomona Catholic Girls High. She thinks school uniforms are a blessing. She likes not having to decide what to wear, which is very good since she is traveling for a year with just a few changes of clothes in her bag.

After highschool she attended San Diego State University (for the beaches) and then Cal State Northridge for a degree in Radio, tv & Film. She then moved to Southern Oregon to begin her career at a daytime only radio station KISD. She thought she was hot stuff earning $700 a month writing radio commercials that a few unlucky listeners may be listening to. Next stint, KTVL TV in Medford, Oregon. Finally tired of the Rogue River Valley, she moves to San Francisco, Ca. Classical music station KKHI is the place. Here, she will be introduced to her future husband, Gary Mex Glazner.

They marry September 29, 1990 and a year later buy his family's flower shop. One year later she will join him there. Its hard work, flowers. They'll keep the shop just along enough before they can realize their dream of traveling around the world for a year.

That brings the poetry widow here, in Paris and Shakespeare &co, and a beneficiary of George's legendary kindness and generousity. Thank you George. This will always remain a highlight of our trip.

Margaret M. Victor
10-29-98

Gary Mex Glazner
Margaret Victor
World Travelers

5 Denise Court
Novato, CA 94945 USA
℡ (415) 897-1554

Little Torito League: How Matadors Get their Cojones

The baby bull rushes the boy, ignoring the cape. The boy swirls the cape to his side. Head down the bull butts the youth sending him into the air, both faces surprised. Instantly dozens of children are on the bull pulling his tail, waving their hands distracting him, teasing him. The bull is confused; he stops and paws the ground sending a puff of dirt up with his hoof. The kids run in circles, shouting, "Here I am little bull, come and get me." The ring is full with 30 or more children. The bull charges one, then another, losing interest, he only wants to be left alone.

This is the chance to try your skill, to play matador. A full grown adult big-daddy bull would have killed. This calf, this bull-child only bruised the fledgling bullfighters pride, taught him a valuable lesson, let him feel the pass, the charge, a head-butt without the stab of the horn.

We are outside of Granada in the little Spanish town of Pelegros, which means danger. This is the fiesta, the bar-b-que following the bullfight from the week before. Everyone is happy, we are eating one of last week's bulls. That is our only excuse, what we tell the Spaniards at our hostel when they say,

"How can you watch the death, the cruelty?"
"We are going to eat them."
They are repulsed.
I ask them, "Are the bullfighters not as graceful as flamenco dancers?"
"They don't kill anyone in flamenco," they say.

We argue back and forth, foreigners against natives. The pageantry, the ritual, the fancy suit, screaming hoards of adoring Chicas. The brutality, the exploitation, the unspeakable worship of blood. Neither side giving in; us with our newfound passion, them growing up with this burden passed down from myth. So we leave it as a draw. They know it is the most Spanish of all things Spanish. We know the infatuation of El Fandi.

The week before we had attended the Corrida, which was being held to raise money for the local school. The Plaza de Torros, or bullfight ring, was a temporary rusted red metal structure. The first time a bull bashed into the side of the ring it felt as if the stands might go crashing down. The high school band was playing the Pasodoble but they were more interested in the chips and soft drinks being passed around and their teacher/conductor had to keep reminding them angrily, "You are meant to be playing not eating!"

Until El Fandi entered the ring, the bullfight for us had been a cultural event, something we thought we should see to understand Spain. With the snow covered Sierra Nevada Mountains in the background, we sipped our beer in the sun. This was a homespun fight, the dead bulls were dragged out by a little tractor, and the crowd shouted to the band if they were playing too loud or at the wrong time.

Our first glimpse of El Fandi's skill comes with the bull's initial charge. Down on one knee, body stiff a perfect line he guides the horns down, then lifts the bull's head up and turns him. The bull stops a few feet away ready for another pass. El Fandi's close to the ground, his body arching as the bull's horns dip down into the cape, gravel and dirt flying with the hooves.

The Picador enters the ring mounted on his horse, lance at the ready. The bull charges the horse. A few feet before he can dig into the horse's flank, the Picador rips his lance into the bull's neck. We can hear the flesh tearing and the blood gushes out matting the black fur of the bull's back a deep glistening red. The Picador leans on the lance, coming off the horse, putting all his weight into the thrust. The bull lunges at the horse. The horse is padded and blindfolded, his sense of fear is tangible. The bull breaks free from the lance, spears his horns into the side padding and lifts the horse off the ground. The Picador regains his advantage jabbing into the gapping whole in the bull's back. The bull pulls away.

The bull's neck muscles are cut, his head hangs down. Now is the time for the banderillas, the barbed ruffled sticks that are used to enliven the bull to bring it back to the fight after the picador's cutting. El Fandi looks up to the President of the bullfight to seek his permission to place his own banderillas. The permission is granted. He faces the bull with the two spears raises his arms above his head, curves his back and dares the bull to charge. He sets the banderillas perfectly, stopping the bull's rush. The next pair are half the size, again the bull is stunned. The last banderillas are six inches long, too short to avoid contact with the animal. An old woman sitting near us shouts, "El chico tiene muy grande cojones!" The boy has very large balls! Everyone agrees.

The boy faces his bull, the bull races, sure of its horns, and the matador is gored. The small spears bounce off the bull's neck. El Fandi walks to the side of the ring, unbuttons his jacket and pulls up his shirt, the crowd waits, the bull has drawn blood but it is only a surface wound. El Fandi returns to the ring to shouts of "Óle" and the waving of white handkerchiefs. The cape and the bull seem as if one, pass after pass, entwined together. El Fandi throws down the cape and sword. He kneels, turning his back to the bull, who is snorting ten feet away. The crowd holds its breath then cheers as El Fandi stands. The bull charges, showing how far he is from death, how much strength he still has. But this is no game of chance, El Fandi has charted every move. He lifts the sword from the sand and kills the bull with one quick blow. The crowd is on its feet cheering, suddenly the band remembers what it is there for and trumpets blare. El Fandi struts around the ring his legs spread wide to make room for his enormous huevos.

Huevos rancheros

The Woman Who Loves Victorian Disease

Karen Hobson loves disease. She first noticed this with the Black Plague. Glowing with her newfound passion of consumption and sexuality in Victorian Literature, she has agreed to an interview with *Ears on Fire* to discuss her thesis. Slightly pale with light blond hair and a gentle cough, Ms. Hobson is dressed in the tee shirt and jeans uniform of the student traveler. We are staying at the Under the Alhambra Hostel in Granada, Spain. The building is old with rough, irregular, whitewashed walls and slanted floors. The interview takes place in the foyer with a wood fire burning. There is a high ceiling with skylight so that the three floors of the hostel open on to the foyer. Through the skylight, you can see the Spanish night.

Ears: "Please tell us of your theory regarding Victorian Diseases."

Hobson: "I love the romanticism of tuberculosis (cough) the fact that Keats died of consumption (cough, cough). I am not the slightest bit interested in modern disease. I know it sounds ghoulish to be fascinated by 19th century disease (cough, cough). We can only hope my cough is consumptive. Consumption was believed to produce interludes of euphoria, enlarged appetite, intensified sexual desire. Having TB was understood to be an aphrodisiac, and to grant extraordinary powers of seduction on the sufferer. The dizzy breathlessness, hectic fever and racing pulse of the consumptive; the glittering eyes and flushed cheeks, night sweats and sharp ache in the side (like an ache in the heart), could clearly convey sexual desire and passion as readily as tuberculosis. However, it is symptomatic of phthisis that many of its signs are deceptive – energy that comes from enervation, flushed cheeks that appear to radiate health but come from fever – and increased vitality which may indicate approaching death, (cough)."

To Fanny Brawne:

My Dearest Girl,

You spoke of having been unwell in your last note: have you recover'd? That note has been a great delight to me. I am stronger than I was: the doctors say there is very little the matter with me, but I cannot believe them till the weight and tightness of my chest is mitigated. I will not indulge or pain myself by complaining of my long separation from you, God alone knows whether I am destined to taste of happiness with you: at all events I myself know thus much that I consider it no mean happiness to have lov'd you thus far —if it is to be no further I shall not be unthankful-if I am to recover the day of my recovery shall see me by your side form which nothing shall separate me, If well you are the only medicine that can keep me so, Perhaps, aye surely, I am writing in too depress's a state of mind-ask your mother to come and see me-she will bring you a better account than mine.

> *Ever your affectionate,*
> *John Keats*

Fanny moves to the window, she looks out onto the darkening field and thinks of the first time she saw him, of his voice which made her warm, the way his eyes spoke to her. I loved him. I wanted his thoughts inside me. Even then he would not be close enough. His words to me, spoken in a tremble, one look at him and you saw the death as if he had a halo, it pulled me, I told myself it was no good, this man was a ghost. How could I know? I will nurse him, fix him, heal him, make love to his light. She slipped into bed and took a poem from her dresser; she traced the curl of the words with her fingernail.

To Fanny

> I cry your mercy—pity—love!—aye, love!
> Merciful love that tantalizes not,
> One-thoughted,   never-wandering,
>   guileless love,
> Unmask'd, an being seen—without a blot!
> O! let me have thee whole—all—all
>   —be mine!
> That shape, that fairness, that sweet
>   minor zest
> Of love, your kiss—those hands, those
>   eyes divine,
> That warm, white, lucent, million-
>   pleasured breast,—

Miles Davis, unknown wanker, Karen Hobson

Fanny put the poem down, slid her hands under the blanket and thought of John, how he seemed to glow. She rubbed his poem every night. O if only he would whisper it to me, stopping the words to kiss, his voice in my ear! When she came to this poem during the day, blushing, she would have to stop and think of something else.

> Yourself—your soul—in pity give me all,
> Without no atom's atom or I die,
> Or living on perhaps, your wretched thrall,

The words were inside her now, she could see John writing them, folding the paper into an envelope, holding it to his lips. She loved the way this poem smelt of hands. Fanny closed her eyes as her breath quickened and warmed her mouth.

> Forget, in the mist of idle misery,
> Life's purposes—the palate of my mind
> Losing its gust, and my ambition blind!

Her lips lingered over the words, holding them in a kiss, as she fell asleep each night, thinking of her lover, so far away in Rome, in his little fevered house at the foot of the Spanish Steps. It is late at night, the fire has died down, we return to the interview.

Ears: "Given your many years of study on this matter have you ever thought you had consumption?"

Hobson: "Once I had a cold and at the same time had strained a muscle in my side so I was sure I had consumption. I told the doctor my symptoms and asked if he thought the diagnosis was correct, and he replied with shock, "My god what have you been reading? You can't get that unless you are a poet living in a slimy grotto!"

Ears: In this culture of skinny is beautiful, it is not hard to imagine the fascination with the wasting disease and super models longing for an ivory tower and a starry eyed poet to lock themselves away with. Although he spoke in quite a different context, we close with a quote from Fanny's love Mr. Keats, "I mean Negative Capability, that is, when a man is capable of being in uncertainties, mysteries, doubts without any irritable reaching after fact and reason—"

The Woman Who Loves Victorian Disease
I carry a small leather bound volume of Keats' poetry. It always comes in handy at bus stops, train stations and airports. After hearing Hobson's ideas on the sexuality of consumption, I read it with renewed vigor.

The Fountain

Black cape
Lace tiara
Red carnation

Slowly up
and down
the plaza

Family strolling

The Fountain
We watched the lovely ritual of strolling take place all over Spain. This poem was inspired by a
morning spent in Barcelona drinking chocolaté and eating churros on a plaza.

Tales from Under the Alhambra

Antonio Phillipe is our leader. In the States his mother, who is an actress and was the first one eaten in the movie *Alive*, calls him Shane. But it is Antonio Phillipe we are interested in as we are in Spain and living in the Under the Alhambra Youth Hostel. We all have Spanish names, which confuses the hell out of the Spanish guests as to why this groupo of gringos have monikers of such Spanish wealth but can only hablo un poco.

Things are well here in this little village of mixed Moorish and Spanish Culture. Have you ever seen the Alhambra? Let me describe a few of its features—it is big, it hangs over the city, a child's dream of a castle, at night it glows like a floating yellow moon. It is where Ferdanand and Isabelle came in 1492 after defeating the Moors. A few miles away in the village of Santa Fe, Columbus made his pitch for the ships and they said no, then said yes, as legend has it on the road to Fuente Vacaros, which is where Federico García Lorca was born. For now I just want to describe the Alhambra to you. Its walls are carved with poems. One staircase has railings of water. If you go, go early as it is always full, for hundreds of years it has been full, with water and the voices of water.

Antonio Phillipe's roommate is Victoria and although you would think that two fine fit young people would be rutting like rabbits, she says no, they are not. Although, we suspect they do naked pushups in front of each other and perhaps tell each other who they do sleep with. Putting the intercourse back in intercourse. Victoria, who can dance a hot salsa, went away with Victor, who cannot. She met him in Up with People, "Up, up with people, if more people were for people than people everywhere, etc." Which of course the Under the Alhambra crowd changes to "Up, up with poets," for my benefit. The best part of being a couple named Victor and Victoria is that people laugh when you introduce yourself even if they have not seen the movie— which I have not. Much like couples in renaissance times must have enjoyed being named Romeo and Juliet. Now, Victor would marry her in a minute, if she was so inclined, which she is not. Her mother sends her email quoting the bible; have you read it? It is the best selling book ever. Although that might have more to do with those obsessive Gideons, than any true literary merit, that and the fact people are scared to death of dying and going to hell, which is not like being Under the Alhambra at all.

Victoria reads her mother's quotes from the bible. What really has her tweaked is her mother sent the email from Victoria's hotmail account. Which means that her

mother has access to her password; which means her mother could have read her email; which means the quotes from the bible about lust and flesh might not be just a coincidence. Since Victoria is in Spain and even though she does not find Spanish men attractive, and wonders how one gender of a people can be so lovely, while the other gender are such dogs, she still finds someone to exchange ice cubes with.

Miles Davis is our roommate with the most famous name. He was conceived while his musician parents were listening to "So What," so they figured "Why not," and named the little baby after the leading cool jazz cat. Miles is British and does play the sax, so each afternoon we drift off on his floating scales and an herb from the Moorish side of town. Oh I forgot to mention that Shane and Victoria are from the States but I guess that was obvious, anyway Miles is always taking a kip, or shagging someone so that is how we know he is a Brit. I suppose we could have just asked, since everyone here under the Alhambra is friendly and gets along except Neb who is gone, and always drank milk and introduced himself as "I'm Neb, N-E-B, I'm a cartographer, that's someone who makes maps." Neb always told everyone what they should be doing, which is ridiculous, since people on holiday never do anything other than what they want to do, which rarely includes acting like Neb.

Oliver is also British, but not posh like Miles, or so he claims, or perhaps its Miles who claims Oliver is posh. Anyway, Oliver drinks the most beer and wine, some times at the same time, and he stayed inside for 72 hours never leaving the couch, to piss Neb off. Then when Neb finally left, Oliver went off for three days on a fishing trip in a town with no river, lakes, or ponds. He didn't catch anything, got home sick and came back to play cards, smoke and drink.

The crew changes every few days. Carmen Maria makes the best paella, teaches us all Spanish and how to eat dinner at 2am. Shawn from Ireland is the funniest person on earth, although with his brogue, I have no idea what he is saying. The worst guests are the Americans who make Thanksgiving dinner and fill their plates with foot high piles of mashed potatoes and turkey depriving everyone else of food and leaving the Spaniards with the impression that being thankful means being first in line.

One night we stage a concurso de vino, or a contest of wine. I cut my hand on a bottle, and Merijn throws out his back. Merijn and Vera are a cute couple from Amsterdam who aren't sure if they want to get married, but know for sure they love Amsterdam and have an apartment so cheap that it costs them more to stay here in Spain, even though the daily rate is around 15 dollars and the wine is so cheap that the most expensive bottle in the contest is 13 dollars, which is 10 times the cheapest. Merijn's back is really out of whack so we fill him up with bowls of hash until he can get proper pain pills in the morning and ride to the airport lying down. The owner of the Under the Alhambra Youth Hostel, Caesar, (which is pronounced THE-sar), wins the contest, with his amazing ability to tell subtle differences in cheap screw top and cardboard box vino. The end result is that wine contests can be muy peligroso.

Most of the people here stay up all night and sleep all day and drink and sleep with someone if they have the chance. Except Margaret and I who have already found each other and like to do things during the day and wouldn't mind people coming with us, only if we asked that would make us Neb-like, so we don't ask. That and the fact that it would be difficult to write down what everyone is doing, if I was doing things. I just want to write to you so you can get a taste of life under the Alhambra. Which is big and beautiful with free little plates of food with every drink and lots of drink and lots of talk in Spanish, since this is Spain and that is what Federico must have felt, rushing around under the Alhambra.

After Octavio

The wind arches over a tall fountain.
Inventing endless bodies for your body.
Touching the yellow earth.
The rooster tears the Sunstone into rivers
of time. Beating out the measure
of your death. Driving you deep;
crucified nail. A golden whirlwind
of words. Paz, little sun
fill the table with permanent noon.
Show us what the orange lacks:
give us your barren tongue
                              noche.

Octavio Paz, 1914-1998
(drawing done upon learning of Paz's death)

Granada

¿Por qué Lorca ha muerto?

As a child they bathed him
        in the red milk of the bull.
When he was a calf they
        turned his horns to the sky.

As a boy he slept in a bed
    of hide.
        The young bull
    fed the grain of bones.

He stands in the center of the
        ring, waiting for the children to sing:
            Today, Today
    we drink the red milk of the man.

The moment
    of forgiveness,
The instant of prayers.
The unbreakable pact.
        How sudden the hooves
    of the riderless horse!

The curious arrive each day.
        Desk empty of poems,
            waiting for the pen's return.
        On the bed a shadow.

Today you are full of children.
    Can you hear them
        from the balcony?
    Can you hear the voices
        coming to take you?

Smell the gun powder?
　　Sweet as assassins eyes.

What will you teach them?
　　How can they know you?

May we use the moles on your face as a map,
　　to find the lost lemon of the moon?

How small these trees must have been when you were a child.
　　Did they shade you as you left forever?

　　Did you ever leave?

The earth holds the molecules of everyone who ever lived,
or ever will live.
　　Each breath we take is full of these uncountable lives.
　　The strum of his poems,
　　　the stomp of his deep song.

　　Olè, forever olè!

He was the filament Edison forgot.
　　He burned so bright the glass burst into a question.

¿Por qué Federico?
Would not old age have killed him by now?

¿Por qué Lorca ha muerto?
I speak to you from the cemetery of animals.

¿Por qué Lorca ha muerto?
Tan Tan
¿Quién es?
 "Soy Lorca,
I hear you are running in circles asking why I am dead.

Why don't you ask me?"

"¿Por qué no me lo preguntas a mi?"

¿Por qué Lorca ha muerto?

Lorca: "   "

Now it is your turn.
You must answer.

Take your time.
   Take time from
   the one eyed moon,
   take time from
ink that is closer to blood.

Seek time
   from all the lovers
     each moment
   they sweat with love.

Place time in the deepest well.

Dip your cup into
the green wet time.

Smell time.

Let it cool
   your mouth.

Let time fill
   your belly.

Siempre tiempo—
　　—Siempre tiempo

You are full with time.

　　Now is the moment to answer.

¿ Por Què Lorca Ha Muerto?

We spent two months in Lorca's hometown of Granada during the celebration of the 100th anniversary of his birth. This poem came out of walking around town asking people why he was killed. It took second place in a poetry contest hosted by the French Embassy and a local language school and was translated into Spanish by Maria Carmen S. Gonzalez.

Pessoa's House Party

The poet is a forger
Forges so completely that
He forges even the feeling
He feels truly as pain
— **Fernando Pessoa**

The Portuguese poet Fernando Pessoa's name translates as Frank Person. In Lisbon you may sit with Mr. Person outside his favorite spot, the café, Brasileria. The faithful have fabricated a life size statue of him at a table having a drink. They have left an open seat. Relax, have a chat, throw your arms around him and give Fernando a big hug. Once aquatinted, we hop on a cable car for a ride over to Casa Pessoa.

Most mornings at Casa Pessoa groups of high school students from all over Portugal meet for a lesson on poetry. Teresa Guerriro who leads the lessons has agreed to let *Ears on Fire* sit in. Teresa has wavy brown hair, a big smile and says, "I use the simple language of students, no big academic words, I want to take off the tie of the poet." Happy to be out of the classroom and on a field trip, the teenagers flirt and tease each other, a strong contrast to Pessoa's imaginary world. Teresa brings them upstairs to the conference room to read from Pessoa's poetry. One of the students sits down at the piano and begins to play soft jazz music, another reads a poem in a strong voice making eye contact with her fellow classmates. For the first time they are all quiet and focused. As the student ends her recitation she receives a standing ovation. Hair bouncing, Teresa leads the cheers for poetry!

Where Lorca is the poet of death, Pessoa is the poet of birth; giving life to full grown imaginary beings, as complex and real as any mother's child. Lorca's houses in Spain are replicas of his existence, complete with family furniture; Pessoa's house is a working laboratory of poetry. Teresa gives them the basics of Pessoa's life. How he created heteronyms; Ricardo Reis, Alberto Caeiro, Alvardo de Campos, and hundreds of other imaginary friends. In fact, the research is not done; Pessoa left a trunk full of poems, 27,543 manuscripts to be exact. Heteronyms are different from using a pen name in that the characters have full lives. Pessoa created astrological charts for each heteronym. The heteronyms would write to each other and to Pessoa's real life friends. Pessoa's one and only girlfriend broke up with him because she couldn't stand Alvardo de Campos. Pessoa replied to her, "de Campos is quite fond of you." The irony of the house full of children, full of people learning Pessoa's poetry, is his lonely existence and his need to create his own world. Now, each day more visitors arrive at Casa Pessoa than arrived during his lifetime.

I ask Teresa if the trunk still exists. She tells me it is housed at the National Library along with the manuscripts. With directions in hand, let's head back to the cable car. Arriving at the National Library, I start to ask about the trunk. I am shuffled from clerk to clerk. It soon becomes clear that no amount of drawing or making shapes with my hands in the air, can convey the idea of Pessoa's famous treasure chest. "We do not have furniture here," the clerk said sternly. They did however take me to the microfilm room and let me study his manuscripts. It is a wonder that any of his writings have come to light at all with his scrawling handwriting. Even with the one step removed feeling of the microfilm, it was exciting seeing the poems as he made them, feeling the thrill of his pen filling that travel-chest.

Back at the café Brasileria, I read in the paper that some students at the university are putting on a play based on Pessoa's life. Shall we go? It is raining when we arrive and there are no signs or directions to help us find the theater. There are two young women on the street. I ask them if they know where the play is being held, they don't, but they are also going. We band together, soon we are joined by more young people, Abdul, Pedro, Franco, Jose, Omid, Luis, all going to the play.

We find the theater and the play has been cancelled. I ask them if they are interested in Pessoa's poetry and it turns out they are poets, who call themselves, "The Living Poets Society." They have rented a cheap room to hold meetings, where they recite their poems, explore life's big questions, argue, laugh and provide each other with a warm sense of belonging, of family. They lead us to a large fountain in the center of Lisbon, we gather together and marvel at the sight of the water arching silver in the spotlights. Creating our own theater.

I ask them why Pessoa wrote in many voices, why he created the heteronyms? They all begin to answer at once:

> "He was lonely."
>
> "He didn't know himself."
>
> "Created friends to fill his sadness."
>
> "As Alberto, he saw simple things, he was happy in every poem."
>
> "He was depressed."
>
> "He created his own world of poets."

They could have been speaking of themselves, or me. We bring ourselves to poetry and see in it what we need to see. I asked them to read me a poem and Carla Lopez began to read in English then switches to Portuguese and let the others translate. She begins,

"Who are you? I'm just a poet."

Ending with,

"I don't know, just dream with something not real."

Then the group fell into a hot discussion. Was the end of the poem to be translated, "not real," or "ir-real?" They liked the sound of ir-real, but was it a word? They went on debating and I thought of Pessoa and how he would have loved these kids so passionate for life and words. How he might have been a little afraid of their love of being living poets.

Later, leaving on the subway one of them says,

"You want to hear some real poetry?"

She quotes from Frank Zappa,

"Listen we can't really be dumb, because its written in this book here, that God made us all just like him. If we are dumb, then God is dumb and maybe a little bit ugly on the side."

The next day as we waited on the tarmac at the Lisbon airport for our flight to London to take off, it became apparent just how proud the Portuguese were of their poet. How much he had entered the public sphere. A plane pulled up next to ours and painted on its nose, was its name, Fernando Pessoa.

The author discussing the World of Poets with the statue of Fernando Pessoa.

Selected Poets, Books, Festivals, and Sites

An incomplete list of poets, books, places and events I discovered during this trip.
I hope these brief descriptions will lead you to seek them out and be inspired as I have.

CHINA

The Dragon Boat Festival—Legend has it that 2000 years ago the poet Qu Yuan, desperate with
sorrow, drowned himself in a final protest against the corrupt government. Each year hundreds of
Dragon Boat festivals take place all over the world on the 5th day of the 5th lunar month. The one
we attended was in Guilin, China.

Mr. China's Son: A Villager's Life, He Liyi, Westview Press, 1993. Autobiography of He's life in China
during the Cultural Revolution. He runs a small café in the town of Dali. While he answered my
questions about Chinese poetry, he was more interested in finding out the best brand of popcorn
for his new microwave oven.

The Silk Dragon, Translations from the Chinese, Arthur Sze, Copper Canyon Press, 2001.

THE CZECH REPUBLIC

For the Love of Prague, Gene Deitch, self-published, 1998. (genedeitch@traveller. cz)
Love story of American and Czech animators living in Prague during the Cold War.

JeJune—Great literary magazine out of Prague (Gwendolyn Albert and Victor Farnsworth,editors):
PO Box 85, 110 01 Prague 1, Czech Republic or PO Box 14624, San Francisco, CA 94114.

ENGLAND

Poet's Corner— Westminster Abbey in London. An amazing collection of memorials and graves
from Chaucer to Robert Graves. Graves was alive at the time of his being memorialized among the
poets of the First World War. When asked if he minded, he replied that,
"I would rather like to attend my own memorial service."

Shakespeare's Grave, Stratford-upon-Avon—Daring anyone to remove his bones, the grave has
this inscription:

> "Good friend for Jesus sake forbeare
> To digg the dust enclosed heare;
> Blese be man yt spares these stones
> And curst be he yt moves my bones"

The Romantic Poets and Their Circle, Richard Holmes, National Portrait Gallery Publications, 1997.

FRANCE

Shakespeare and Company Bookstore—Located at 37 Rue de la Bûcherie, in Paris.
*Fire Readings, A Collection of Contemporary Writing form the Shakespeare and Company Fire Benefit
Readings*, Franks Books, Vincennes, France, 1991.

GREECE

Angelos Sikelianos *(1884-1951)* "We've got a language...we're still making it, it's a language for
poets, not for shopkeepers. Listen to this— and he began reciting another poem, in Greek. That's
from Sikelianos. I suppose you never even heard the name, what?"
Katsimbalis in Henry Miller's *The Colossus of Maroussi*.

Angelos Sikelianos, Selected Poems, translated and edited by Edward Keeley and Phillip Sherrard, George Allen and Unwin Press, London, 1979.

George Seferis *(1900-1971)*—Won the Nobel Prize for Literature in 1963. Born in Smyrna, an ancient city on the Aegean Sea, thought to be the birth place of Homer.

On the Greek Style, Essays and Poetry, George Seferis, Denise Harvey & Company, Limni, Evia, Greece, 1982.

Aristotle's Poetics, Hill and Wang, New York, 1961.

Greek Woman Poets, translated by Eleni Fourtouni, Thelphini Press, 1979 New Haven CT

The Marble Threshing Floor, Studies in Modern Greek Poetry, Philip Sherrard, Dennis Harvey & Company, Limni, Evia, Greece, 1992.

HUNGRY

Arany: Poems and Drawings, Arany Janos, Miklosovits Laszlo, 1997. Not translated into English, but the drawings are amazing.

Any poems by Miklós Radnóti.

NEPAL

My Discovery, A Book Length Poem, Banira Giri, translated from Nepali by Yuytusu R.D., Apurva Publications, Kathmandu Nepal.

Modern Literary Nepali, Michael Hutt, Oxford University Press, 1997. The motherlode of information on Nepali Poetry.

Nepalese Literature, A Journal of Nepalese Writing, edited by Shailendra Kumar Singh.

Anonymous Fathers and Other Poems, Tek B. Karki, Himalayan Concerns Infonet, 1998.

PORTUGAL

Fernando Pessoa *(1888-1935)*—His name translates as Frank Person. In Lisbon, you may sit with Mr. Person outside his favorite meeting spot, the café, Brasileria. The faithful have erected a life size statue of him at a table having a drink. Best known for his creation of Heteronyms, literary alter egos given complete biographies, politics, aesthetics, and religion. He even created an astrological chart for each creation. Pessoa left over 25,000 manuscripts written by over 100 Heteronyms. His home has been turned into a working museum/poetry library. Each morning classes of kids from all over Portugal visit the Pessoa House for workshops on the poet.

Casa Fernando Pessoa—Rua Coelho da Rocha 16-18, P-1200 Lisboa (telephone: 3968190 fax 3968262).

Fernando Pessoa, edited by Maria José de Lancastre and Antonio Tabucchi. Wonderful bio and photo book on Pessoa's life.

Always Astonished: Selected Prose, Fernando Pessoa, edited and translated by Edwin Honig, City Lights, 1998. Find out about Sensationism and the genesis of heteronyms. "If you ask me to explain what the state of my soul is, assuming there's a sensible reason, I'd reply by pointing silently to a mirror, a hat rack, and a fountain pen."

Sapa—A small café in Sintra, an easy train ride from Lisboa. They have poems printed on hand made paper hanging on the walls and delightful bite sized cheese cakes. (telephone: 9230493)

Thailand

Thai Literature, An Introduction, Klaus Wenk, White Lotus Co. Ltd., 1995.
G.P.O. Box 1141, Bangkok, 10501

Spain

The Alhambra—Floating above Granada like a child's dream of a castle. The walls are decorated with the beautiful scrolled Islamic poetry of Ibn Zamarak. His poetry praises the construction and the builders.

The Penguin Book of Spanish Verse, edited by J.M. Cohen, 1998 Penguin Books.

Federico García Lorca *(1898-1936)*—A poet, dramatist, musician and artist. Studied in Madrid along with fellow student Salvador Dali. Lorca was executed in the early days of the Spanish Civil War. Simon Andrews hosts in-depth tours of Lorca sites in Granada including his family estate, "Huerta de San Vicente," birth place in "Fuente Vaqueros," and the Federico Garcia Lorca Memorial Park," where it is believed Lorca is buried.

Lorca Tours in Granada—Simon Andrewes, telephone: 958 123 575 or 958 818 852
Postal address: c. Ecuador 20, 18007 Granada, Spain (simo@arrakis.es)

Vietnam

Spring Essence, Ho Xuan Huong, translated by John Balaban, Copper Canyon Press, 2000. The first collection of Ho's poetry available in an English translation.

Viet-Nam, Civilization and Culture, Pierre Huard and Maurice Durand, Paris Imprimerie Nationale, date uncertain. Great section of Vietnamese poetry

The Quiet American, Graham Greene, Penguin Books, 1955. Knock off copies of this book are sold on the street all over Saigon.

Colophon

Set in *Vendetta*, designed by John Downer, distributed by Emigré.
Vendetta can be classified as a Venetian Old Style typeface, though not a revival
but a fresh reworking for contemporary usage.

"My fascination with historical Venetian types began in the 1970s and eventually led to
the production of my first text typeface, Iowan Old Style. Sometime in the early 1990s,
I started doodling letters for another Venetian typeface, one I constructed geometrically.
The letters were pieced together from sections of circles and squares. The **n**, a standard
lowercase control character in a text typeface, came first. Its most unusual feature was
its head serif, a bisected quadrant of a circle. My aim was to see if its sharp beak would
work with blunt, rectangular, foot serifs. Next, I wanted to see if I could construct a set
of capital letters with serifs to match the rectangular lowercase serifs. Rectangular serifs,
or what we today call "slab serifs," were common in early text types cut in Italy before 1500.
Slab serifs are evident on both lowercase and uppercase characters in roman types of the
incunabula period, but for most lowercase letters they are almost always seen just at the
baseline. Exceptions are **v**, (**w** came late), **x**, and **y**. The head serifs on lowercase letters of
early roman types were usually angled. They were not arched, like mine.
Oddly, there seems to be no actual historical precedent for my approach."

Titling is *Mercator*.

Book Design by J. Bryan.

Gary Mex Glazner makes his living as a poet. He is a graduate of Sonoma State University's Expressive Arts program with an emphasis in poetry. In 1990, Glazner produced the first National Poetry Slam in San Francisco. Glazner is the Minister of Fun for Poetry Slam Incorporated. In 1997, Poets and Writers Inc. awarded him a grant to work with Alzheimer patients using poetry. Glazner won the individual series in the first Poetry Olympics held in Stockholm in October 1998. From November of 1999 to June of 2001 Glazner was Poet-in-Residence at the Inn on the Alameda, in Santa Fe. The hotel gave away 45,862 poems from his Southwestern series. Glazner edited the anthology entitled *Poetry Slam: The Competitive Art of Performance Poetry* (Manic D Press). Glazner organized SlamAmerica, a poetry bus ride across America, which featured 37 readings over 30 day period in 32 cities. The tour took place in the summer of 2000 and over 100 poets participated. Glazner is the director and executive producer of a documentary film on the tour. The film, *Busload of Poets*, was selected by the Santa Fe Film Festival and had its world premiere in December 2001 on opening night of the festival. Glazner along with Amalia Ortiz won the 2001 Tag-Team Championship vs. Quincy Troupe and Pat Payne at the Taos Poetry Circus. In the spring of 2003, Sherman Asher Press will publish Glazner's book, *The Road Less Travelled: How to Make your Living as a Poet*. Glazner born was born in Oklahoma in 1957. His middle name, Mex, is shortened from New Mexico. His great-grand parents homesteaded in Stanley, New Mexico in the early 1900's and named their son Mex. The name has been passed down since then. He lives outside of Santa Fe with his wife Margaret and their dog Federico.